KU-529-815

THE
LIGHT
IN THE
DARK

THE
LIGHT
IN THE
DARK

A Winter Journal

HORATIO CLARE

First published 2018 by
Elliott and Thompson Limited
27 John Street, London WC1N 2BX
www.eandtbooks.com

ISBN: 978-1-78396-404-8

9 8 7 6 5 4 3 2 1

A catalogue record for this book is available from the British Library.

Typesetting by Marie Doherty
Printed in the UK by TJ International Ltd

To Rebecca, with love and gratitude

PROLOGUE: SUMMER'S END

The last days of August were beautiful and the nights ethereal, glowing long after sunset. In Wales, on a glittering morning of dew and high whisks of cloud, the sun hot, Mum and I walked in the meadow by the stream, Apollo running circles and barking as if he were still young.

'The Russian proverb goes, "Life is not a walk across an open field",' I said. 'But it is sometimes.'

My mother, hugely smiling, repeated, 'It is sometimes!'

We looked at the hill, our mountain, rearing over the valley. 'The bracken is on the turn,' she said. Pale ribs like shadows ran under the green ridges.

We agreed we loved this change of season. The swifts went weeks ago. I saw them on an afternoon that was steamy with rain, hunting over the valley, twenty, thirty, and I knew they were going. Swifts come and go like spells. I watched them keenly, lucky to witness them just before they went. It is not the same with swallows: all over Europe and Eurasia watchers look up one day, or pause in thought, and realise that the swallows have gone. We all know what it means.

It is early September now, back in West Yorkshire, where I live with Rebecca and the boys (our son Aubrey, five, and Robin, his brother, sixteen), and I am looking for the swallows. I have seen them go as late as October in Wales, but here in the North of England I have never marked the moment. Two days ago I thought they must have gone; Rebecca has seen none either. Then yesterday, coming back from the seaside – the coast of Lancashire, a-dive with kites and aglow with sunburn – I saw some from the train, two or three over a stubble field, and cheered.

The train was old and packed. We could have been in Bulgaria, with the heat and the flushed faces and the children crammed between us; but at any time and in any country it was unmistakably one of the last trains on the last weekend of the summer.

This week the schools go back and the new year, the working year, begins. September is easy to love. I feel alive in the weather, in the light and the colour. Aubrey and I looked at the leaves this morning. On the Buttress, the wooded hump of hill which fills the view from this little house, the solid green is gone. Now there are many greens, all of them riching or fading.

'Soon they will be yellow and red and orange and brown and gold,' I said. 'And then the leaves will fall.'

The first blew off the trees last weekend. If it were followed by spring or summer, I would love autumn unreservedly. Even the absence of the swallows and swifts and martins would be fine: they will come back, and they must go if the world is still to turn. But for all its gilding, I shrink slightly at autumn, as if I too lose leaves and thin, because I have come to fear winter.

Now it is after midnight on September 5th, my birthday. There are tiny black midges biting me in the attic; they are doing very well still and it is too muggy to keep the windows closed. It was a day as hot as July, yellowing greens like moulding broccoli and vapour greys, a wonderful thick, warm atmosphere, and I am thinking about winter. I loved the winter, with its miracles and Christmas colours, for years. Through school, through university, through first jobs, proper jobs, through years abroad and in Britain again, I relished it as I did all the seasons. Only in the last three or four years, here in the North, have I begun to admit that winter is tough. There is the weather: the black rains make you feel you are living in a tunnel under the sea, the roof leaking downpours; there is the enclosure of the moors, turning you in on yourself, shrinking the scale of life to a few small rooms, the dank and the dirty trains. There is the absence of light and the feeling of living in an ugly country, streaming roofs, weeping windows, dank inside and out. All over the North we experience these sensations which gather and spread like damp. In Wales the skies set in, 'crows-on-posts weather' my mother calls it. Commuting in London is weeks, months, of grease-water running down the steps of tube stations, and buses like Louis MacNeice's 'Charon':

> . . . at each request
> Stop there was a crowd of aggressively vacant
> Faces, we just jogged on . . .

Last winter I thought I would go mad with depression. I was mad, but aware-mad, at least. Sometimes I hung out of my attic window, staring at the Buttress and the sky at the end of the valley with incredulity, waiting for the awareness to go and leave me raving.

It was nothing inexplicable: depression brings fear, entrapment, fault and failure wherever you look. The book I was writing seemed awful and I could see no hope: if I cannot write, I cannot support my family, cannot be the father my son deserves – so the narrative goes. It is not fair to blame the winter, but it does set the stage so well, with its clamped-down rains, its settled and introverted darkness, its mean ration of light, its repetitions.

But this year will be different, it must be different. This book is to be a torch raised against it. I will take it down in notes and diaries. I will embrace this winter like a summer. I will try to see this little shard of the North as I would an unknown country. I will pay attention. Depression kills your power of vision, turning you fatally towards yourself, but I will practise looking and looking outwards like an exercise, as though I am training for an expedition. Mountains make sense in any weather. The voices of a wood always speak consolation: the trick is to resist the psychological deafness, that bung of jeering voices clogging the inner ear. Beware that glaze which creeps over the inner eye, blinding you to the brightness of moss in rain. I will not lose touch with nature. This is vital. I believe in immanence, in the oneness of living things. Maintaining that faith will carry you through the hardest times. Or such is the hope, this midnight. I start my birthday with many wishes, and this is one.

16 OCTOBER

Last week I saw two swallows, halfway down Wales, fine-tailed birds flicking against the wind, hunting. Late-breeding adults, they will have raised two broods. On their way now and travelling, they will not really stop anywhere long. In a month or so from now they will be around the Congo and Cameroon, twinning the world, linking every raised head and every eye that sees them. Today was astounding, courtesy of ex-Hurricane Ophelia. There was a pink Chinese silk balloon sun in a mustard sky. It looked like a portent, if not the apocalypse. And I saw a hobby! They should be gone, but she seemed large and fit, slicing over the town. If you can catch swifts in level flight you can catch anything, and there was plenty around. A sparrowhawk was up there too; it mock-attacked a pigeon which burst out of its tree in a fluster. All the birds seemed to be up, riding the currents. Later the sky cleared; there was sun and tremendous wind in a blue rush over the moors. It was a pale-white whirl of light over the plain towards Manchester and Liverpool and Wales. I turned my face to hot sun-wind (we had sun-rain a few days ago, when it seemed to be raining light) and watched jackdaws in storms over the high woods, rolling in black sparks on the breakers of the sky.

I take down these moments in the middle of driving, commuting or ferrying the family, consciously sealing them into the visual memory. 'Look hard! Take a picture with your mind,' I say to Aubrey as we practise his letters. It works.

17 OCTOBER

The first sniff of winter! There was a hardness about the white dust in the lines of the road-stones, and there was that smell, a coldness. Winter colours came suddenly, in slightly slanted light. I shivered. It was warmer later, but for the first time in months I chose thicker socks.

20 OCTOBER

On Wednesday afternoon in Liverpool the Anglican cathedral seemed to float, to lean back, to descend. I teach Creative Writing in the city, two days a week in university term time. I love to teach, and I have colleagues I adore. The trudge to work and back is vicious: over two hours each way on trains, but when the weather is kind you arrive in Liverpool's clear air to sea light and gull cries. Now the colours were pure winter. Grey as glumness. Kerb-coloured sky, and about the buildings a hard pallor. There were three tiny luminous figures like money spiders on the cathedral tower. 'It's like a climbing centre,' my friend Jeff Young said.

You rarely meet a man as beloved as Jeff. A playwright, screenwriter, essayist, performance artist and gentleman of letters, Jeff is tall and very thin, mercurial and gentle. He believes in love and magic, in always learning. He says things like, 'I never had a job until I was sixty,' and he reads generously, constantly, always looking for the good in a work. His heart is huge: he carries all of us in the department, staff and students, because he lives the example of what an artist is and what a good man is – intensely kind, aware, curious and paying attention. Jeff has a rebel's sense of justice and injustice, history and change. He believes in and practises the artist's role in disruption and radical engagement. He is almost physically appalled by bullshit of any kind, which makes his relationship with the managerial jargon and culture of the university machine entertaining to witness. 'I've been sent this *email*, right,' he will begin, incredulously, and then his eyes will meet yours over the tops of his glasses and you will both start laughing. Thank God for Jeff Young.

Jeff, like me, is seasonally sensitive. He loathes Christmas as much as he loves his family and being with them. They are going to Prague this year. Movement and change are good remedies.

Studies have found Seasonal Affective Disorder affects around 6 per cent of the population of the United States, with another 14 per cent experiencing a dip into winter blues. It varies with latitude, of course, so in Oslo rates are much higher, approaching 15 per cent. Victims sleep for an average of two and a half hours longer than they do in summer, and they struggle to get up. They eat more, particularly sweet and starchy foods. They have difficulty concentrating and withdraw from family and friends.

An expert in the field, Norman Rosenthal, pins the condition to lack of light. People with a genetic predisposition, he found, may experience the same symptoms at any time of year if they work in basements or windowless offices. The building where Jeff and I work might have been designed to induce it: gloomy, crushing architecture, with windows that seem to repel light rather than attract it, where the available food is a combination of starch and sugar. We loathe it, the students loathe it; when we discovered that it stands on the site of the Liverpool workhouse, we decided the psychogeography of the place must have something to do with its miserable atmosphere, as if the desperation of old souls seeps up through the floors.

22 OCTOBER

It is early hours of Sunday morning, rocked and thumped by Hurricane Brian. Why do they goad the winds with these comical names?

For the last three days there has been wind strong enough to snap thick branches and the leaves are falling in armies. I worry it is going too fast, this high autumn. Alarming bareness strings through the trees, between all the leaves of couple-colour. The raptors have been up; everything has been up. Pigeons riding the gales like fat darts; buzzards, kestrels, jackdaws of course, missile-tip starlings and gulls, gulls, gulls.

The drive down through Wales in the teeth of Storm Brian was wonderful today. Flags and sails of cloud that should have been horizontal blew diagonally, filled like spinnakers, and they were all colours: mauve and torn grey, scratched pale blue and wuthering white. It was as though the wind was the souls of the dead, from Shelley to machine-gunned Liverpool Pals to Leonard Cohen, ganging up like rowdies, commandeering taxis, racing through the air.

25–30 OCTOBER

The end of October flicked from joy to horror as quickly as you turn a page. The 25th was a luminous day. I was coming to the end of teaching on a writing course at Ty Newydd, near Llanystumdwy. My co-tutor, Jon Gower, has the rosy face of a young wizard who will one day be impossibly old. You have never seen eyes brighter or more mobile. His voice is the most beautiful Welsh instrument. It says things like, 'I know of a woman who was the last person in Montgomeryshire to hear fairy music.'

In a trade in which extreme productivity is only slightly unusual, Jon is a constant forge of books, articles, poems, short stories, fiction, essays and monographs. We spark and light each other. We go at the teaching all-out, and our students are a treat; it is one of those miraculous courses where the experience and the curiosity in the room are dizzying, where humour and openness rule the week, where the whole group flies forward into reading and understanding and writing.

In convoy we drive to the end of the Llŷn peninsula, where the cliffs scoop down to the sea. Bardsey, the isle of saints, seems to float on the seven currents which beset it.

We get the writers to describe Bardsey, to paint in large strokes. We have them study the starred colours of the hedges and render the minute world in detail. We watch choughs and ravens, gulls and rock pigeons. The light is almost indescribable, a great flaring silver-gold kindled between the sky and the sea, a singing, blinding beauty.

'If you want to find God,' Jon says, 'you just have to come here and look, don't you?'

We return, our spirits lit bright by the day.

I feel joy and hope, and love for Jon, and deep gratitude for these days, these days of life. This is the happy time, I tell myself. I am superstitious about happiness. I worry that too much celebration of immanence, of God-goodness and life force, invites its opposite. Some pagan part of me believes that too much light draws darkness.

After dinner, the whole party of us in celebratory mood, I open a message from a friend, Dai Morris, with whom I was at primary school in Wales.

Please pass on my apologies to your mum. I saw her this morning and had to pass on some bad news regarding her sheep which had been attacked by a dog (presumably). As I drove by there were two maybe three dead ones and a few very badly injured. It was a horrific scene and one that I really feel for her having to deal with. It wasn't the time to have a chat so please pass on my sympathy. All the best, Dai

There comes a nauseous thump in the gut, and the sudden, hard drum of the heart as the world narrows, my vision tunnelling. I call home. My mother's voice normally is full of intelligence, curiosity, life and playfulness. Now she sounds twenty years aged, a wavering old lady adrift in confusion.

'Badger-baiters,' she says. 'They set the dogs on them. The vet's been, she put three down. We think they killed Sorrel with a fence post.'

'I'm coming,' I say, 'I'm coming. I'm on my way. I will be there very soon.'

'Drive carefully,' she says, 'please drive slowly.'

At first, I do drive very slowly. Think clearly, I tell myself, be calm. You must be very calm. No accidents, no mistakes.

Carefully, numbly, I drive to Criccieth, to Porthmadog, to Dolgellau. It is a still and misty night and cold, as if autumn is out there in the dark woods, whispering with winter. At Dolgellau the roads empty. It seems just me and the car, crossing a deserted Wales. Somewhere in the twisting passes between Newtown and Llandrindod a rage bursts in the pit of me, a howling, violent thing exploding, and the furies come screaming out, and I roar in the car.

My mother is in bed shaking, in shock. I pile on more covers and try to be very calm, very soothing. She had been on a course in the morning, so the two dead sheep and the three savaged and dying animals were not discovered until Dai saw them and found her. She called the vet before going to the field. All the ewes had torn throats, some also had broken legs. Two dogs at least had been used. Just behind the trees of the fence line the badger setts had been dug, three fresh holes – a deal of work, and, if each gave up a badger, lucrative.

This is the season when the sows have cubs: they will fight anything now. A badger sow is worth a thousand pounds to the diggers, who will run the fight in some barn, some shed or quarry. Dogs will be set on her and bets taken. Some clans of these diggers call themselves terrier men, and are associated with hunts. They send a terrier with a tracker on its collar into the setts to corner a badger. Following the signal, they dig straight down and lift the animal out.

'When I went around them last night I noticed one ewe looking at the hedge,' Mum says, 'but the leaves are still on and I couldn't see what she was looking at. That's where they were, just there. They must have been watching.'

Four years ago she ran a group of baiters off our land. They hurried away, concealing their faces, leaving behind a terrier with a tracker on its collar. Mum took the dog home and called the police. The police made enquiries and told her the men wanted the terrier and the tracker back. They said these were frightening men. They advised her to have nothing to do with them.

The police have been here again today. One, a male constable, did not want to climb over the fence into the field. He was worried about tearing his trousers. The other, a woman officer, managed to cross the fence – my mother, in her late seventies, crosses it every day – and she took pictures. The police told my mother that they had not kept records of the men with the terrier and the tracker.

It seems likely they do know the perpetrators: the baiters use certain dogs, pit-bulls crossed with lurchers, which must be hard to miss.

For four years the badger-baiters bided their time, then struck, confident in their impunity. The message is for my mother, first, but for the whole valley, too.

'It was the way the ewes looked at me,' Mum says, 'they'd been waiting so long for me to help them. I will never forget the way they looked at me. The vet put three of them down.'

She has something like a fit while we are talking, a fit of shakes and gasping. I soothe her and talk to her; eventually she calms.

I drive to the murder field. There is an absolute silence and blackness beyond its fence. I know the shed is piled with dead animals. There is a complete dark nothingness there, something utter and eerie, a nihilism, a nothing you should not be able to feel but cannot mistake. I patrol our other fields, and the valley, and the other setts. From my earliest days of childhood in Wales I remember Mum talking of badger-baiters as if they were bogeymen: cruel, warped people who might come on a winter night, whose torches might be seen bobbing through the bare trees, who sometimes left us intimidating messages – a glove hung up by the middle finger, a dead badger thrown into a shed.

I stand at the entrance to the shed, looking down on the still and staring eyes, the torn throats, the blood and the ripped and bloated bodies. I say a silent prayer, and the refrain of Patrick Kavanagh's great lament for love which brings pain. It was love of the animals and love of the valley and love of the life of the open air which hurt us now, much more than any thug's abuses.

. . . let grief be a fallen leaf at the dawning of the day.

Let grief be a fallen leaf, I think. There is much to do. And indeed, in the days that followed the winds blew, the leaves fell and winter's occupation began.

4 NOVEMBER

As November stubs out the glow of autumn and the days tighten into shorter hours, we make decisions. We will not lamb this year. As a tribute to and a lament for our slaughtered animals, we decide not to put the rams to the ewes, to take a year off. Mum needs respite. We retrench and plan and it is still a desperate time. The horror of it haunts us.

'I took on the farm because Amos who sold it us said you've got to have sheep, and here's a flock, but if someone had told me they were as sensitive and empathetic as Labradors I would have thought twice, frankly,' Mum says.

To come home to find a dog butchered and dying in the living room is perhaps the nearest a non-farmer can come to imagining her feelings. I go to church, partly to see my neighbours, and partly for something else.

'As we forgive those who trespass against us,' keeps running through my head. Do I forgive them? I think I understand them. These are people of the margins, clinging to a thrill which may have come down to them in many ways, from a time when the countryside was rich in animals and birds. If they are terrier men, associated with hunts, as investigators believe, then their pleasure is only a version of the kind that the fox-hunting fraternity have always enjoyed and wish to see reinstated. Their dogs, the pit-bull—lurcher crosses known as bull-lurchers, are terrifyingly indicative of their masters' state. Awkward, bizarre creatures, mus-cled like bulldogs, swept and lifted like lurchers, mutant descendants of Cerberus, short only of two heads, they are for killing – and if you were the

25

kind of person to own such a dog, wouldn't you want to see it in action?

For you, winter would be a thrilling season. You would plan and plot, study the moon and the weather and the map. Loading the tools and the dogs, timing the run, finding the parking place in the right gateway: this is adventure. And the hunched hurry along the fence lines, and the hiding, and the watching, and seeing your victim come and go and miss you: this is defiance. You have slipped through; the world now belongs not to farmers and shepherds – it belongs to the outlaw, to you. And the digging and the fighting, and the trapping and the lifting, the imprisoning and the bagging-up, the squirms of your prey and the darkness all yours – what a night!

To top it all, to make this a bit special, to have something extra to confide to those who thrill to the gossip of what you do, who come to the fights, who laud you – why, you set the dogs on the old woman's sheep, of course you do. You love it as much as the dogs do.

11 NOVEMBER

We keep going down at the weekends; Rebecca and Aubrey come too, to help sort sheep, to inject, treat and move them under Mum's direction. Her recovery is astonishing and wonderful to watch. I come in one evening to find her in her dressing gown, her nightly whisky-and-milk in one hand, the phone in the other. She is issuing instructions and advice to a neighbour. She looks alive, decisive and vibrant, like a general.

Preparing for winter has its own rhythms, as old as our exchanges with the land. November 11th, St Martin's day, was the time when medieval farmers assessed the balance of livestock and hay. Every animal over the number that could be fed was slaughtered and salted. Abbot Francis Gasquet's close reading of the accounts of the priory of Grace

Dieu in Leicestershire gives a glimpse of how the nuns prepared for winter. In early November salt was purchased, and tallow and mutton fat, ready for the visit of the candle-maker, whose rush-lights and cresset-lights would, as Gasquet put it, 'have done hardly more than make visible the darkness of a winter evening'.

We move the sheep to the lower fields and haul feed to the shed on the mountain. Mum goes into long negotiations with repairmen over the wicks for the cooker. It is the heart of her house and very old, performing the same function as the fire in the calefactory, the common room, sometimes 'warming place', of a monastery. These were lit on the feast of All Saints, November 1st, and kept going every day until Easter.

Hill farming is mostly a battle, but in the winter the rules change. You are not worried about flies and maggots, now, and less fearful of disease; the cold brings that relief. ('I saw C. V. Wedgwood lecture at Cambridge,' Mum says. 'She was a great expert on the Civil War. She said that the night after the Battle of Edgehill in October 1642 was bitterly cold, a really hard frost. It meant that the wounded soldiers didn't get infected – the cold saved them. Casualties were much lower than they were in summer battles.') With the leaves gone, the sheep are easily seen; they cannot slink off out of sight if they are ill or in trouble, which is their habit. They need feeding with hay, nuts and mineral blocks, and they need water. It is gruelling work, for even if he or she is ill or carrying an injury, a good farmer can never miss a day.

Growing up on a hill farm, the winters of my childhood were a jarring of cold gates, the frigid iron biting through your gloves, the cut of hay-bale string in your palms and the rock of frozen mud beneath your boots. My brother Alexander and I loathed the cold but relished the winter: in bad years snow cut us off for weeks, which was the greatest adventure for small boys. We hoped for snow as ardently as our mother dreaded it. There were amazing weeks in which the farm became a ship trapped in ice. We walked down the hill in the morning to the car, and then back up in the evening after school, our mother having done another up and another down in the interim, and fed the sheep. Following the lane through the wood was like a frigid safari. Here were the lopping tracks of rabbits, here the tiny trails of mice. Rooks roosted on the road in the leaf litter on very cold nights, leaping out, cawing purple as we approached.

My mother kept her coat on in the house. In the old days the animals were stabled beneath the farms' sleeping quarters, their warmth rising through the floor. In Tibet I saw the same system still in use: Tibetan farms are like castles, with a high-walled forecourt where the pigs are fed, and wide planks forming the first floor with gaps between them only partially plugged with straw. You can look down and see the cattle moving below you. You smell them and hear them, as if every farm is Noah's Ark.

18 NOVEMBER

Winter in the mountains is arresting in its drama, the light melting over the Brecon Beacons as though it carries cold in it, not heat. There are the lakes of mist, too, the sun riding high over the bracken-red ridges as they surface through pearlescent cloud, heaving up like whales. Winter by the sea is another kind of theatre, like standing in a great and empty auditorium. The first time I moved back to Wales from London as an adult, I had been living in a boat on the Regent's Canal near Marylebone. The boat had no hot water: I took showers on the towpath until it became absurdly cold. Then I looked for a vacant holiday cottage, somewhere far away and as cheap as possible, where I might write.

I found it in Little Haven, West Wales, a village in a crook in the cliffs where a stream runs down to the beach. There is a stickle of houses, a cove and a promontory, all but deserted in winter. Only the path, a hip-high wall and the wedge-end of the cliffs separate the cottage from the furthest reach of the sea. Every wave, at high tide, slaps and shushes under the windows of Beach Cottage. After storms, sea slaters came in under the door; I did not know what they were, these giant sandy woodlice, but I laughed and talked to them as I ushered them out, being short of company. It was a strange and lovely place to live alone, a holiday cottage in off-season: the only other neighbours were ghosts and builders in dispute over the renovation of the pub next door. At low tide you could walk two bays north to the shop, oystercatchers your escorts along the strand, skittering and piping through the foamy unfurlings of the waves.

The winter sea seems to have little time or thought for land, as though its soul is elsewhere. It flattens and gathers, coldly preparing its storms, withdrawing its colour, leaving shades and tones, hiding its lustres and tints behind its grey back, showing them elsewhere, no doubt, on some blue-green shore. The sea does not call to us now, as it did and will again. Only the seal-silhouettes of the surfers go down to the water, black hoods bobbing in grey waves. The introspection of the sea is almost frightening in winter.

Small tankers and coasters taking refuge from the weather come to anchor in the bay, their arrivals and departures unseen, shuffled by mysterious callings. At night their lights and the noise of their generators come clearly across the water, seeming to speak of their isolation, the unknown ports of their voyages, as though their travels link obscure shores and shelters into a chain of unmapped littorals, countries existing only as marks on the fringe of maritime charts.

Great storms and downpours march in across the Irish Sea, and icy mornings, and there comes one extraordinary day when mist covers all the land but breaks in pastel ridges of pink and pearly valleys over the shore, so that the sea is clear and the coast an archipelago of blue vapour, floating above itself.

It was a striking winter: I was writing a book and recovering from shocks I did not understand. It took me a while to find names and shapes for them. One night, in the dim front room of Beach Cottage, I realised I had been in grief. A relationship had ended months before; only now did I understand how and what I had lost. I had gone through parting from the other person – that had been months of pain, borne together, and then apart – but not until that moment in the salt-damp house by the winter sea had I admitted and understood the loss of the third figure, the love between us.

The refusal to acknowledge pain seems very male now. It is bizarre that I could have gone so far into that winter, so far to the end of the land, without really knowing what it was that ran with me and inside me. Surely women are closer to themselves, more able to sense their own tides? And more self-aware men are, too, no doubt – though there is a gender gap in self-knowledge and admission. The realisation seemed to change everything. I exclaimed aloud. It was as though someone had sat me down and said: Listen, you have been heartbroken. That is what this is. The migration to the winter coast made sense, then. In turmoil we are drawn to water, to space, to the high places and the wider views. It must be a very simple reflex: a need for escape and perspective which weather and landscape fulfil. The sea has a power to draw out and rearrange our anxieties in simpler patterns; on the coast paths and the empty beaches I found a deep untangling. There is this in winter, too, in its reductions and parings, simplicity.

I moved to an empty house belonging to a friend in St David's, the smallest city in Britain. In summer it is in permanent spate, flooded through with holidaymakers. For a few weeks in winter it transforms. Now a Welsh-speaking population rejoices in their own tongue; you hear the curling spells of the language in the mornings before the vagrant visitors arrive. Tapping with hammers down the twilight lanes, St David's makes its way through the winter, preparing for the next season. The radio picks up Irish stations, as though we are not on the western fringe but instead an island, the hinterlands of Wales like a sea behind us. Before us, out there beyond the horizon, some Celtic mainland lives, speaking and singing in the accents of the oceanic West.

St David's surrounds the cathedral, a most lively and animated marvel, with its showers of jackdaws, the mauve and purple tones of its tower and the motions of its anchorage. Hidden in a valley, it sits like a ship in harbour, the flexing waves of the ridge trees riding behind it in the wind.

Without visitors, unpeopled, the cliffs and headlands return to their creatures. At St Ann's Head a buzzard surveys her planet from a fence post. What minor orders of life are all things under that small imperial gaze! Near Martin's Haven the choughs tour their peninsula, unafraid and miraculous in glossy black plumage like dress uniform, joyfully paired with beaks and legs of clown-scarlet.

Sea mists like enchantments cover the land, stilling all sound, returning the nights to deep silence.

15 DECEMBER

In high pressure the air itself seems to recede, as though the cold fires of the stars and the moon draw further away, leaving a vast, deep bowl of freezing, exhilarating, space. The early mornings with their slow dawns are beautiful. There was a brush of frost, then two days later a white freezing. At daybreak the meadow below the lane was frosted, leaving a handsome dark border, unfrozen, running under the trees where the field reaches the beck. I was beginning a long journey and the taxi driver was delighted by the cold: 'It's minus two!' he said, in the way we might exclaim, 'Twenty-eight degrees!' in summer.

'Look! Winter!' he said, pointing at our neighbours scraping their whitened car windows.

As the train crossed the viaduct above the roofs of Todmorden the whole town was steaming, the vapour from boilers and showers curling in perfect focus into the frigid air. There was much goose business abroad, gaggles gathering on the Rochdale Canal, and small skeins of the birds, Canada geese, flying over Smithy Bridge. I wondered if the cold was bringing flocks from further north down to join the locals, or if the first snap energises them the way it does us.

Further along the canal, heading for Manchester, with the light widening and tautening as it does just before the sun makes his entrance, three horses picked up their feet as they trotted along the towpath by a lock. Everything about them was alive, their movements skittish, palpable energy in their quick steps, as if the ground was tingling under their hooves. In Manchester's Victoria Station a slightly haggard Santa selling *The Big Issue* did not look incongruous in the cold. He gave his 'Ho-ho-ho!' to commuters with genuine amusement. When the sun did come, it threw a blinding gold glare across the plain between Manchester and Liverpool. Small ponds and plashings were frozen coins.

There have been ominous sunsets like spilled fire under brooding cloud, and in daylight the bare trees reveal the country and its creatures in a clarity the other seasons deny. Cold winters do away with claustrophobia, and they are a gift to birdwatchers. We watched a great spotted woodpecker at work on a branch which frosty moss had made emerald. He looked immaculate in black and white, red cap feathers and his scarlet undertail coverts like flashy boxer shorts. In Welsh lore the dragons still thrive – they have merely taken the form of green woodpeckers. The whole woodpecker family have something dragonish about them. They may not have arrow-head tails, but they do have extremely long tongues, for scooping bugs out of holes in tree trunks.

It does not do to romanticise drizzle, rain on motorways, months of strip-lighting, office windows black at four o'clock, concrete skies, sock-damp, rain-prickle, mould-steam, deadbeaten fields, sodden livestock and the chilly tug like foot-sucking mud that winter can exert upon the spirit. But the cold does offer great compensations, like the subtle colours, the days as bright as a magpie's cackle, and those stretched tones that bruise the blue of a cold sky in its fading.

17 DECEMBER

We make preparations for Christmas. Rebecca buys Aubrey a Lego advent calendar. Every morning is a lesson in numbers – he has to find the right date – and a joyful opening of windows, yielding small figures and machines. 'Look Dad, look!' His joy infuses all of us. When will we get The Tree? When is Christmas? How many days? Is it tomorrow? What will we eat? What will Father Christmas bring? How will he get down the chimney?

Our season is hauling firewood, drying clothes, lining the radiators with washing, stuffing boots with newspaper, layering on jumpers, keeping track of Aubrey's vests, celebrating different versions of Rebecca's homity pie, ferrying Robin to and from the station, always in the dark. Robin is running the full gamut of the standard train chaos in his commute to school. One week, he says, not a single one ran right. I order a goose. We obtain and decorate the tree. I find I even enjoy Christmas shopping (I hate shopping, normally), buying presents without counting costs. I have made money this year, with radio work and articles and books and teaching. In the back of my mind is January's tax bill, but I push it into a corner. I am a fool, a happy fool, putting off the days of reckoning. There is another side to the season, like a slow drum. Jenny, Rebecca's mother, works at the food-bank in Rochdale. She says it is busier every week. The news keeps getting worse: child poverty, NHS crises, a dithering government, the prospect of an insane and disordered Brexit. There is a despairing feeling among my students, caught between anxiety in the present and fear for their futures. You can hold it all off and 'crack on', as Rebecca puts it, but to think about it at all is to confront an ominous gathering of bad signs. Cheerfulness and the responsibility to be joyful, especially for the children but for everyone you meet, seems on the one hand a quixotic duty, almost a wilful blindness, and on the other a vital celebration of the moment, of the now.

24 DECEMBER

On Christmas Eve Hebden Bridge gathers to sing carols in the square. It is Rebecca's favourite night of the winter. We moved here, when we had to return from Italy, because we needed to be close to Rochdale, where her son Robin's father lives, and because Hebden is beautiful in its way, and alternative: gay, cosmopolitan and left-leaning, with music and moors, woods and a Steiner kindergarten, which Rebecca wanted Aubrey to attend. They do Christmas unrestrainedly here: there are hay bales around the tree, a brass band in toppers, children on shoulders, and high up, like small, cold angels, pigeons on rooftops, gazing down.

It is as cold as it should be, and as the carols start the faces of this singular Pennine town rise, tilt and give voice. This is the only time you see them all. It feels as much like a solstice as a Christian festival. Here are farmers, whose tractors seem to keep the town honest, roaring in muddy splendour down the main street, and the mason-builders, like my friend Mike, whose handshake is a grip like warm stone. There are the locals, like Lyndon, our neighbour, God's Yorkshireman, whose red MG is the emblem of our lane, and who seemed to take to me straight away because I arrived here from Italy in an old Fiat. Lyndon says 'brass' the way only a Yorkshireman can say it. He runs the beaters for the moor shoots, teases Rebecca about coming from 'that dark place' (Lancashire) and is the soul of the Blue Pig, the working men's club in our valley, which looks like a Hobbit inn by the beck.

Here are the 'offcomers', crowds of us, who have migrated from the cities for the air, the moors and our children, for the beauty of the skies, for each other – Hebden is an island of Southerners in the Pennines – and the promise of working remotely. Here are the writers, the photographers, the teachers, the lecturers and the BBC crowd who commute to Salford.

And there is Frankie, soft-spoken and pale and watchful, who came from South Africa. 'I was never safe before I came to Hebden,' she said. She speaks very quietly. She fled bigotry, not crime. 'This is my refuge. It's the best place in the world.' The town's lesbian community is famous, and a decisive advantage. 'Hebden's full of project managers and alpha women!' was one of the classic lines to come out of the devastating flood of Boxing Day 2015, when the town rescued itself in a surge of giving, volunteering, donating, organising and rebuilding.

Here is the Trades Club crowd, lined faces and pints and laughter, and here are the smart jackets and boots of the lawyers and bankers whose Jaguars (for the men) and Range Rovers (for the women) sigh them to work in Leeds and Manchester well before the light. 'Good King Wenceslas looked out', we sing, 'on the feast of Stephen!' And there are to my certain knowledge atheists, pagans, Buddhists, agnostics, theosophists, Catholics, Anglicans and at least one Sufi among us, flushed and loud and even.

Leading our section – which is Aubrey, our friend Dawn, her three children, Ember, Piper and Luna, and Little Frieda (our dog, a black Labrador compiled of love, greed and folly) and me – is Rebecca, her face lifted and lit with amusement and happiness. Rebecca is a tide-race of different currents: intensely community-spirited and also shy, friend and mother, teacher and partner, runner (ultrarunner), forward-directed to an amazing degree, slob and beauty, intensely moral, hesitant sometimes, ferociously qualified and learned. We are singing carols because she loves this ritual. She is a pagan, she says: the kind of pagan who will sing in a Catholic choir, for the fun of it.

Before Aubrey goes up I check that the chimney is ready for Father Christmas. The little boy is bouncing around, springy with thrill. What a privilege it is, later, to wrap presents and hang stockings. Rebecca and I go to bed as excited as the boy. I have caught myself saying, 'I love Christmas!' several times in recent days. Rebecca, Robin and Aubrey have given it back to me, after years during which I rather dreaded the downpour of commercial nonsense, and the logistics – Wales and Rochdale, and Robin divided between his father and us, and spare rooms and sofas, and getting back from Italy and then back to Italy on overstuffed trains and aeroplanes.

25 DECEMBER

Christmas Day is sleety and unpromising and no one cares: we have the tree and the lights and torn wrapping paper, toys and clothes and books. We drive over the moors to Rochdale, a mottle of sleets and rains falling.

Jenny, Rebecca's mother, says she settles down with a book when the sun makes it warm enough to sit outside 'about once a year'. The house is a sparkle of lights and tints, shining glass and polished cutlery. Christmas Day in Rochdale is a pressing-on of drinks, a turning-out of best clothes, a procession of traditional food – pâté and melba toast to start, always – and a constant, loving mockery.

We are a medley of voices, Rebecca's soft Lancastrian, her family's broader Rochdalian, Robin's Mancunian, my RP and Aubrey's Yorkshire. Aubrey and his school friends have developed their own dialect: light is 'loit', right is 'roit' – it is impossible to resist imitation.

The families of Rochdale are serried over the contours of the moors and the town; Jenny and Gerald and their children and grandchildren are sewn into a tapestry of near-family and friends. There is 'the Cricket' – the cricket and rugby club – and the schools (Jenny, a governor of the primary where she taught, can name generations of children and their parents), and Gerald's golf, and the lives of their friends, the aunties and uncles and cousins. These are networks of deep understanding, knowledge and sympathy. Meals and gatherings here unwind over timeless hours of gossip, concern and cross-reference. Auntie Emma is teased about her nights out; Uncle Chris about his looks (he is saturnine, bearing little resemblance to his sisters), which leads to Jenny being teased. Rebecca is teased because she always has a rant about the NHS, through which we all try not to roll our eyes: Gerald was a hospital porter in Rochdale at one point, and Emma is high up in NHS management. I am teased for attempting to cut Aubrey's hair – he came out of it looking like a tuft of sedge – and Gerald will never miss a chance to mock my Welshness. Robin is teased about his love life (he is devoted to his girlfriend), and then we go around again.

It is a long, gentle day of feasting. There is no tension, no argument. I feel a blissful love for this family, whose culture is so unlike the one I came from. My brother and I were formed on a mountain where our school friends were half an hour's drive away, our cousins an hour and our father three or four. We were a mighty little army, the three of us, and the dogs and the cats and the mice behind the wallpaper, the sheep and the wild creatures, but we have been diffuse ever since I went to boarding school at eleven, my brother following two years later. Wales is for us a redoubt, a return, our hearts' land and our mother; a place both memory and wish.

26 DECEMBER

On Boxing Day we drive south and west. The country is upside down to Northerners; they know North Wales better than I do, but the South is a long haul. I relish the drive, alert with the hope of taking Rebecca back into a landscape I have always loved and wanted her to love, and the happiness of bringing Aubrey to his other grandma, Grandma Sally. They have a deep and mischievous connection, and astonishingly similar looks and expressions.

It is not an easy drive for Rebecca because she and Sally have clashed in the past. They will be cordial and kind for as long as they can. At some point, over a mishearing, over politics (they are both left-wing), over education (Sally was a teacher, Rebecca is one), over child care (they are both indulgent and loving mothers), and probably towards the end of an evening towards the end of our stay they will flare. Winter and Christmas bring this trial on them both. They are valiant in their attempts to resist it.

'Hello Sally! Happy Christmas!'

'Hello Rebecca! Happy Christmas! Come in luvvie, come in, was it a very long drive?'

'No-o, it was fine really . . .'

They are, at least, warmer to each other than they have ever been. In a rainstorm I watched them walk uphill together, close in conversation, and my mother put her arm around Rebecca, just briefly, and Rebecca swayed towards her, reciprocating.

'How are you honeybun?' Mum asks, her most affectionate appellation. Their joint endeavour to get on is wonderful to witness. Over Aubrey, they are as one.

'Don't give it to him now,' I protest, as Mum produces a thick chocolate cookie after supper, 'he's just about to go to bed.'

'Well I'm allowed to spoil him because I'm his grandma,' she returns, with a wrinkled nose for me and a twinkle for the child, flourishing a fat fragment.

'Thank you, Grandma Sally!' he chirps.

'Is that most delicious, Bug?' his mother grins.

'Oh let it be a child's Christmas in Wales!' I wish, and it comes true.

It is cold, properly cold; Rebecca and Aubrey take refuge in the bowed bed of the guest room, while I sleep on the sofa. We need electric blankets and blasting heaters to make the attic habitable the following night. Below the mountain we dream, and I am there again.

The mountain is a white whale and the lanes are lined with ice. The trees have stars in their branches and all the fields sparkle. The night seems to listen to the owls' carols as the dogs growl in their sleep. The spirits are abroad. It is Christmas. Christmas! Was there ever such a magical word to a child? A word with a world in it, a word containing a silver moon and the crackle of burning twigs, flying things and kings led by stars, berries and gold and pheasant feathers. A word with the darkness of fir forests in it. As a child I knew the spirit world, shapes pushed into the corners most of the year that chased me upstairs, hung around in the dark by the door and lurked under the bed. There were dragons on our mountain and ogres behind the lowering clouds of winter. My mother, brother and I lived close to them all, high above the valley in an ancient farm – we had bats and rats, tame mice and huge spiders; goblins would have been no surprise. But only once in four seasons did the adult world stoop to enter the one we lived in, and what a cascade of marvels there was then.

'Christmas is coming . . .' our mother said. Everything was coming. Our father, whom we rarely saw, would come, and Father Christmas, whom we still had not seen, and food, feasts with puddings, which we never had, and presents. We would even, in our aunt's house, see some television. Indiana Jones, Darth Vader and adverts! We loved adverts.

The advent calendar provided the drum roll and then it was upon us, and at last the grown-ups dropped their miserable obsessions with school and work and bills and turned to matters of true importance.

'We're going to get the tree today!' our mother said, and we cheered. We lived in the coldest house in the world, but at least we had the biggest tree. It came from old Mr Berenbrock, who had been a

German prisoner-of-war interned in Wales and had stayed. Somehow it seemed right that we should get the tree from him, as though peace had just come again and we were still playing football in no-man's-land.

The tree had tremendous power – spiky and delicate, sticky with sap and that smell, like a strange relative who came to preside over the best day of the year. With the lanes too icy to drive on, we carried it up the hill and dragged it over the meadows. It was the first really green thing the sheep had seen for months and they piled in, ravenous.

'Oh hell!' our mother cried. 'Lift it up, we'll have to run.'

We dressed it like a god in lights and glass and tinsel. When it was done we turned off the other bulbs and contemplated it, bewitched by its colours and shadows, the infinite and tiny worlds in the baubles and the spaces between its branches.

'Now for the holly,' she said. 'It should be good – as long as the fieldfares haven't eaten all the berries.' The coming of the northern thrushes was another sign, like the fire's embers in the morning, that the great feast was near. Out we went again, to the copse where the fox lived and the pigeons roosted, to do battle with the spiny trees.

'Why do we have holly?' I asked, as the prickles jabbed and scratched us.

'It's supposed to be to do with the crown of thorns, like the Yule log has become the Christmas tree – Christmas comes from an ancient pagan cele-bration, a festival of light in the darkness, renewal and birth in the death of the year.'

We were natural pagans, my brother and I, we dreamed of feasting and fighting like Vikings and hoarding treasure (unwrapping presents was the climax of Christmas for us, the bit we knew we should not look forward to most of all but did, and with the stockings it came twice), and we loved the season's stories. Christmas was a blizzard of stories, a world transformed by their power, and we made no distinction between the ancient and recent.

Behind the bulging wallpaper in our bedrooms were Beatrix Potter's mice, scrabbling and making nests with bits of thread. The back of the wardrobe in the freezing spare room had never been seen, hidden by our mother's old clothes. Dresses and coats and flares queued in there, packed like bodies in the tube, costumes she never wore now that she was a farmer and single: 'going out' meant going out to the sheep. The wardrobe smelled faintly sweet, of unknown things brought closer by Christmas: London parties, her life before, as distant and romantic as frankincense and myrrh. No one could say that a lamp post in a snowy wood and a lion and witch did not exist behind them.

T. H. White's wolves pressed their red eyes to the keyhole of the front door as the flying Snowman passed high overhead, towing Aled Jones through skies thronged with angels, guiding lights and sleighs; in the mornings there were hoof prints all over the snow – reindeer tracks among the sheep's droppings.

At Christmas, after we had gone to bed, our mother said, all the animals could talk. The sheep would moan about the cold and the food, of course, because all sheep are always hungry, but I wondered what the old cat hissed at our dog. What a rattle of conversation there must be down there, as the mice compared notes on their ordeals in my trap, a cereal bowl propped on a pencil (I always let them go) and the cat asked the dogs for a quieter year, please, less midnight barking (it was eerie and terrifying when they did it for long, baying like wolves to the moon), and the dogs told wild stories about all the foxes they had nearly caught and the badger-baiters they had seen off.

The badger-baiters, sheep-stealers, sundry weirdos and the spectral breed my mother called collectively 'mad bombers' could all be relied upon to stay indoors on the special night, so only kind spirits haunted our mountain. If the dogs barked on Christmas Eve it was a good sign, not a threat.

I thought of shepherds, even older than our neighbours, on another mountain, wondering what marauder troubled their flocks as the miracle approached. With no television to confuse us with pictures of what was actually happening in Manger Square, all time seemed to roll at once.

The streets of London would be silent, I imagined, except perhaps for one or two men whom my mother had watched, once, laughing and shouting because they had never seen snow. The shipping forecast was the last thing I heard. Out at sea somewhere, Tintin and Captain Haddock sat in the wheelhouse of a rusty freighter wearing paper crowns and sharing a bottle of grog.

The voices from the radio, our only regular visitors, would bring us familiar but honoured guests. Tomorrow, the Pope, speaking in seventy tongues, would wish us peace on earth. Tomorrow, the Queen would say, 'and a very happy Christmas to you all' in exactly the tone she was using now with Father Christmas, no doubt, as he laboured up and down her hundred chimneys, filling all her stockings with parcels.

There were two Father Christmases: our own, who was there when we were very young, and who came on Boxing Day after the divorce, and the crabby old man created by Raymond Briggs, who slithered down the chimney, cursing, blooming this, blooming that, no less real for his present-buying partnership with our mother. One year, when our father was still there, I woke in the dark before 6 a.m. and led my brother down to see if He had been. Yes! The lumpy, serpentine weight of stockings was proof that all the stories were true. Anything is made magical when wrapped in an old sock and a myth. The lights went on and our parents peered groggily from their bed as we extracted our treasures.

My brother, in a flurry of enthusiasm, tore into a pack of playing cards, ripping the box in two. 'Careful!' I squeaked, sanctimonious prig. 'Remember the poor Africans.'

'Oh shucks,' our father groaned, 'at least they can get some sleep.'

He cooked a goose that year with the head still on. The eyes turned into raisins and the beak looked like yellow crackling. My mother has not eaten one since.

In the following years, when he came on Boxing Day, our Christmas doubled while our mother's was halved. He took us away in the evening for a miraculous annual week of shows and television and radiators and lights and the countless Christmas trees of London, leaving her among the decorations and the torn wrapping paper. She never let us see how it must have felt. 'I'll be fine,' she said bravely. 'I'll be just fine . . .'

In the middle of everything, though, between the stockings and the presents, was 'the point of it all', as my mother put it, which meant frenzied hair-brushing and a hunt for decent clothes to go with our new jumpers. Church became more engaging as we grew up. The village beauty would be there again, we reminded each other, and there was always a good sermon.

Our rector had something of a druid about him: sacred white hair, deep, bright eyes and the high Welsh voice of a poet. He welcomed us all very warmly, gently wry in acknowledgement of our influx. Sometimes he asked us to think about Light, but the best sermon was on the Word, the Word made flesh, the Word from which all things came. The Word that was God and with God and the same in the beginning: it was hard to follow. As a pantheist and pagan child who had not made up his mind about God, church meant carols and readings, cribs, the journey of the Magi if you were lucky, and Christingles, which were oranges with candles in them. I never expected, at the height of the Christian year, to be gripped or moved by faith, but one midnight Mass it happened.

As we sang and kneeled and prayed, in the third pew the rector's wife sat or stood, out of time, helped and comforted by her children. Her face was bewildered, strained and confused. She was fast in the grip of Alzheimer's. They had been battling it, but the fight was nearly lost. The rector loved her with all his heart, and his heart, we could see, was breaking. But he carried on, carrying her, carrying all of us with him, his thin voice wavering as he preached that year's sermon. The subject, he said, was Joy. He spoke of joy to the world and the need to be joyful, the responsibility on this of all days to feel the joy the Christ child had brought, and the need to spread that joy around us. I do not think I have ever witnessed a man do something so difficult, so brave and so terrible. The rector and his faith were in the furnace before us. And though joy was not, and hope was not, and whether you believe it or not, God was there with him. Even a child could see it.

27 DECEMBER

Now our child wakes and demands action. We surface slowly, reluctantly, but soon Rebecca is jumpy for exercise.

'Come on Aubrey, boots on, Mummy needs her walk! It's like living with a panther, isn't it?'

'Or a T-Rex!'

'Let's take our T-Rex out.'

We drive to Castell Dinas, a humped and almost perfectly conical hill that commands the pass into our valley. It is a fairy hill today, white, thick-crystalled and glittering. We climb slowly through banks of fortifications. At the top there are the low remains of a gateway, and then, below and before us, the whole of the valley and the mountains rising, the nearer ramparts running up into cloud. The course of a stream – marked only in ticks and scurries of black rock – descends out of the vapour, stitching the sky to the flanks of two huge ridges in a single stippled line. The valley runs south, the fields yellow-green below the snow line as the light reverberates between the hillsides. Aubrey bustles along the battlements, slaying foes. Rebecca's legs are barely stretched but she has air and height around her, and she is laughing. Uncle Alexander stands and absorbs. Mum's normal habit is to see and exclaim – the instinct to cry, 'Look, children!' has never left her. But sometimes she stops, still and alight with a view of the world, and shakes her head, speechless.

Our mountain forges through blue below higher cloud. It is astonishing, seen from here, frozen, swept-peaked and towering. In the distances below there seems no end-stop, no horizon, only the hills rolling down to far away, to the speckle of trees and farms and the fair lands of the lower Usk Valley, their hill fields shaded across in brightness where sluggish winter grass meets vaunting white.

The contours of this view and the snow's power to change it are unaltered by time. From the Iron Age at least humans have stood here, felt the tiny surge of energy in the winter sun and faced eternity, as near as we can conceive it, in the lines of the mountains and the moving cloud.

You can feel our time on the summit in the snow as a scene hung in memory's hall as it unfurls. Perhaps the transience of the snow lends it this quality, a needful, fragile, moment-to-moment beauty, and the five of us here, and all well, and happy. The summer of 1978 is under our feet, when we came up here for my fifth birthday, and there was a camping trip at the turn of the millennium when I slept up here, and there was an expedition in the 1980s with the girls from the farm down below, when we caught newts in the plashings between the ramparts. Each time is vivid. There is some power in this outcrop, some line through time. I bet anything Aubrey will remember it.

10 JANUARY

In the blue dark of the morning the sky is a luminous dim indigo. Schoolboys pick their way through white slush. A girl with no coat hurries to the station, dressed in skirt and tights. These are tough people. Thin wisps of birdsong come through the bare woods and I am aware of gathering every sign of life and nature, as though assembling charms and touchstones against a lowering threat. A crow mobs a heron over the valley field, and on the canal Canada geese seem to glow, their soft colours enriched by snow-light. The skies are capricious and restless, throwing down combinations of hail and sleet, raining slush. Under the trees the woods are patched green and white, the thickets and trunks feeble and bare, as though they cling to the earth on probation.

On the way to work, on the train to Liverpool, I watch a thin sun struggling low under the lid of cloud. Dear old Britain! Bits of it look superannuated, fit for abandonment or bulldozing. We pass housing intertwined with spoil heaps and rubble, rusted wire and litter, enduring under dirty skies.

We pass Rainhill. I was amazed by the names of the North when I first came here, the heavy, cold poetry of them, names with hard skies in them, flat and dully gleaming like broadswords. Brown Wardle and Rooley Moor Road; Hardcastle Crags, Blackstone Edge and Syke. The Cemetery Hotel waits for a novel to be written about it. Rainhill made its almost forgotten name long ago. A mile of the line here, which is perfectly flat, was the site of the Rainhill Trials in 1829, when Stephenson's Rocket defeated all its competitors for the nascent Manchester to Liverpool Railway, co-fathering the Industrial Revolution. The Rocket hit a top speed of thirty miles an hour, faster than my commuter train seems to be able to sustain. It creeps between stations, pausing as if it forgets its mission every few minutes. I think of the great cities, of Shanghai and San Francisco, of Paris and Berlin. Compared to life in them this is medieval, as though we live in an eternal winter, a geriatric country, small and hunched inwards, talking irritably to itself. And yet there are stipples of buds on the ash trees, and more birds than you would ever see in Italy. We pass a primary school and the whole playground leaps and dances with children, hooded and gloved, bouncing like lambs.

The wide plain between Manchester and the coast has been combed bare by the cold, the bracken a dead, reddish tangle, the oaks gaunt. Small lines of sheep feed on a scattering of swedes. I remember my parents doing the same for our flock when I was very young, one of those absolutely clear memory flashes of childhood like a snatch of perfect footage in a bleached-out film. I can still smell the tubers; I can still hear the rattle of our neighbour's tractor and feel the unforgiving ground. Edward Thomas, a man who knew well the torments of winter and depression, and the tearing pull between making a living and creating art ('I dragged him out from under the heap of his own work in prose he was buried alive under,' said Robert Frost, who was partly responsible for turning Thomas to poetry), saw the same work in the fields, and hymned it, in the winter of 1915.

SWEDES

They have taken the gable from the roof of clay
On the long swede pile. They have let in the sun
To the white and gold and purple of curled fronds
Unsunned. It is a sight more tender-gorgeous
At the wood-corner where Winter moans and drips
Than when, in the Valley of the Tombs of Kings,
A boy crawls down into a Pharaoh's tomb
And, first of Christian men, beholds the mummy,
God and monkey, chariot and throne and vase,
Blue pottery, alabaster, and gold.

But dreamless long-dead Amen-hotep lies.
This is a dream of Winter, sweet as Spring.

Winter as a moaning, dripping spectre, a ghost untombed, unhoused, and the swedes as a treasure hoard, transfiguring winter's spirit with an epiphany of colour, texture and accumulation: what attention, what strength of soul, to catch the uplifting moment. Thomas suffered terrible depressions. To follow his eye across the three winters of his poetic outpouring is to walk with a companion in constant negotiation with the ghoul that moans and drips at the wood-corner. It is so easy to feel for him and with him that it is hard to read him.

I am aware of an inner fighting, of a struggle not to lie down under the battering of these dim, thudding days. I am hiding in forced cheerfulness, and earlier bedtimes, and eating more sugar – pouring down muesli and honey on toast. The symptoms of seasonal depression are all there and I cannot shake them. I catch Rebecca's assessing eye, and I can feel her strength, as if she spreads her shoulders, taking on more of the burden of lightening the house and making us all happy, as

I retreat into obsessive washing-up and hear my voice starting sentences with 'No' and 'Don't'. The negative is taking up residence in me, like mould, like rot, like decay.

The Calder Valley, where we live, has a high suicide rate, ascribed to 'Valley Bottom Fever': the feeling that there is no way out, and that real life, life and laughter and excitement, is very far away. The reasons for living here are good, but in the darker time I seethe with the conviction that all life and my life is passing in the rain and I have no means of controlling it or changing it. There are many, many who feel this way all over the country, but the moors and the in-twisted geography of the valley do have a potent way of focusing it.

I am very bad in the mornings. We hold it together until we get Aubrey to school, then some glum comment from me, some hopelessness will spark between us, and Rebecca will flare. It is dreadful to live with the depressed, and astonishing to live with someone dealing with it as Rebecca does.

Sometimes an argument will run until 09.29, when she will switch on the camera and microphone on her laptop and begin work – she is a senior teacher at an online high school, instructing students around the world in Classics and English. Her voice switches from battle mode to charming welcome in a second.

'Good *morning*, everybody! Are we all in? Let's go around – tell me the weather where you are today . . .'

I love listening to her teaching. Her immense capacity to love and support zigzags out across the ether, to Saudi Arabia, to Hong Kong, to Spain. Like the very best teachers, she changes lives with every lesson, through tireless assessment and understanding. She turned herself into a Classicist in between her job, the house, the family and marathons, retiring to bed with Aubrey and another black-covered Penguin translation of Homer, Ovid or Euripides. He can tell you all about Pegasus, Perseus, Medusa and the 'Kwacken'.

18 JANUARY

It always snows on Aubrey's birthday. This year we had hail in drifting swirls, then came eerie sleet, filling the valley and all the air with an army of ghost legs marching too close together. The snow fell later, and it was heavy and fast. By nightfall it was inches deep. Rebecca and the boys took an hour to cover the mile up the hill from town, the road being blocked with stuck cars and a gritter which slid into a wall. Action and incident are the best possible salves to depression: bring on the big snow! Bring on disruption, bring on change; bring on anything to take me out of my (increasingly self-loathed) self. I love weather like this, weather that overwhelms, subordinating all human plans. It lays white, thrilling drifts over the gloom. It forces you into the present, and reminds me of adventures, of battles on the farm and explorations in the Dolomites, when we lived near them, and of the greatest adventure of all, Aubrey's birth. For his birthday we had a feast of duck legs and pasta and birthday cake. Aubrey's face was all delight in the glow of his five candles as we sang him 'Happy Birthday'. He is still distressingly taken with nuclear bombs and missiles (he spotted a gap in the market when he asked for a toy nuclear bomb) but, as my father says, it does not matter what you are interested in so long as you are interested in something.

Five years ago, Rebecca gave birth to Aubrey on a snowy night in Italy, in Negrar, a town in the foothills of the Dolomites. He was purple when he emerged, and yowling, and the most beautiful thing in creation if beauty is fragile and raw and mighty. Just as she was going to bed at quarter past ten Rebecca's waters broke. At the hospital there seemed to be no one else in the maternity unit at all, just a midwife and her assistant. The midwife had a face of the most extraordinary beauty, the beauty of pure kindness, I thought, the beauty of absolute empathy. In Italy they register the name before the child is delivered. 'Ow-bray?' gave the midwife trouble and amusement, 'O-bray?'.

We were taken to a room with two beds, both empty, where Rebecca rode the contractions, bending, breathing, breathing. Before she took up marathons she performed yoga daily. Now she seemed to rock and sway and bend and breathe through a mazy course of pressures and pains. I imagined them like tides, like the blown branches of a dense forest, forcing her to duck and bow to their surge.

We moved to the delivery room and an orange birthing pool, something between a jacuzzi and an altar. There was a back-lit ceiling decorated as a sky with cherry blossom. It seemed incongruous, afterwards, with slicks of blood swirled down the steps and across the room to the bed where Rebecca recovered.

They put a monitor on her to measure the strength of the contractions. Ten would have been a more severe cramp than most men have ever had. It went up to 120 three times. She seemed to see the size of the pain the second time; she shouted, this mighty woman who surrenders to nothing, she shouted, 'God! No!' and in a broken way that raked my heart, 'No! Please!'

I had never seen a human in such pain. In impotence you stand there, feeling her agony through you like a slash when she screams, like a spear of distress for her so strong it is almost physical – but only almost. All your agonising equates to a bare iota of discomfort, and she screams. She squeezes your hand and you wish she could crush all the pain into you. I felt the awe of a heathen, an animist who has worshipped in woods, who walks into one of the great cathedrals. So this is the height and complexity of what it can be, of what giving life is, of what the burden is; this is pain and creation.

The third contraction came with a great groan and then she was gasping, and the midwife beckoned, 'You can come and see him!'

I said, 'I'll stay with her a moment,' because she was holding my hand tight and it felt wrong to rush to this new being while she was as she was. And then he was. An uncurling body almost out, and then out, making a furious noise, with his bright-blue umbilical which looked so patterned and strong and superb it seemed like some flawless artificial tubing from some sophisticated machine. I cut it, as Italian fathers do. It is a thin symbolism; from the moment Rebecca first held him they were more than two individuals, they were two parts of a third, a whole, a united being.

The stern swaddling nurse handed him to me and departed, and as she went she smiled at us, the only time her face shed its fierce cast, a radiant smile, as surprising as a blessing, Aubrey's first. Rebecca held him to her, colour slowly returning to her face which was white, her eyes black-circled with blood loss. She put him to her breast and he slept. There was a rocking, hypnotic peace about them both.

No one came. We took him back to the room. He was yellow now, a touch of jaundice the Italians say is common in winter babies, and tiny, and so tired. He slept beside his mother. To hold him, so new, so small, made me feel like a tentative giant. The tiny, mole-like utterness of him, in his little clothes too big for him, and the feeling of a compliment greater than any you have imagined when he sleeps in your arms, and the sheer impossible vastness of everything ahead of him mantles your shoulders over him. You are all newborns together, you and him and the world, which seems quite changed by his arrival.

On this first morning of his life I went out to buy nappies, wipes and baby oil. Negrar stands on the side of a valley with vines and foothills all around. The horizons were patchworks of purplish and bare trees and snow; the church bell rang the hours and I had never seen a bleak daybreak so beautiful.

The feeling of life, of new life, of all our new lives rushed through me. I thought the man in the café must have seen men in my state before, newly hatched from the delivery room and silently beside themselves.

Beyond the window of our ward men laboured in an olive grove, paring the branches, puffed and shivering as they worked in the cold. It was as though the governing of the trees on one side of the glass and the nurturing of the children on the other were all one great goodness of humanity, tending and gardening.

Fathers were not supposed to stay in the hospital but they let me, that night and the next; I propped myself between the chair and the bed. Two days later we took him home.

Then and afterwards I came to know the small, tender conspiracy of smiles men permit themselves and each other in maternity wards, in corridors and waiting rooms. We were all perpetrators, it seemed; we had done this thing and the results were beyond our imaginings.

It became a blessed and blessing winter. Aubrey and Rebecca took long baths. We laid him on cushions and blankets in front of the wood stove; we were living on the top floor of a villa, which must have seemed huge to him when his eyes began to focus. I escorted his brother to school in the early dark on buses which were never delayed by snow.

Robin and I laughed at the surrealism of our lives, so much in darkness, so much in cold, and all in Italy, as though we tunnelled to school through a world of misted windows and boot-tread patterns of snow. In the short daylight the beauty of the frozen valleys was intense, ridges of white and mauve in a tinted chiaroscuro. High above Garda the great peak of Monte Baldo was a white giant's head, visored in ice and rock.

The cold scours out the Veneto, scrubbing Venice to the minimum of visitors and thickening the colours and lights of Verona. Winter here means sweet panettone and darkening fogs trapped between the mountains and the sea. It means the warmth of trains and the cold of platforms, and hard blue soaring days. It means winter tyres and winter kale, and downfalls of snow skidding under the street lights.

With Aubrey arrived, like a miniature immigrant from another planet, we saw the whole world anew. We talked to him all the time, describing common things as if we had never seen them before. Beyond the windows in the courtyard of the villa was a mighty cypress tree with a missing crown. I thought of it as a great green god, and I took him to see it often, hoping he would smell its dark sap. He lived in a world of pure expression, beyond the limits of language. His iterations of joy were absolute: lying on his back he whirred and gurgled, waving his arms and legs. Rebecca's mothering of

Aubrey was – is – a manifestation of love and self-lessness like nothing I had ever seen. I knew she was a total, giving, mighty mother: Robin was just turning seven when I met them, and her devotion to him was absolute. There is no patience of which she is not capable, no battle she will not fight, no limit to what she will do for her child. But with this tiny, dependent and yet deeply individual little life attached to her, I saw something else. Sometimes in the middle of the night, for the third time, the baby would wake her and she would sit and feed and nurse him almost in her sleep. From the first moments of his life he can only ever have been certain that there was a warm, soft, comforting being, love made physical, with him, for him, always. She talks to him always, loves him always, is there for him always. In watching them, I saw the fundamental bond, belief and trust upon which all humanity must be founded.

19 JANUARY

The struggle is intensifying. It is like being sealed into a grey snowball which keeps gathering defeats. However much I wash, I seem to smell of dirty winter trains and exhaust. The eye desperately seeks beauty and light, but winter is a miser at the moment, giving nothing but bills. The result is inarticulacy. Facing a lecture theatre full of students, I cannot entertain, digress and make them laugh, as I hope to normally. The words and the lightness will not come. Instead I write everything down first, and work through it carefully and slowly, so that I will not be left gulping in silence. The working, connecting, creating brain seems to shut down completely, leaving a dirge of an inner monologue that will not shut up about failure and mediocrity and guilt. There are many moments in seminars when I realise, with gasping relief, that concentrating on the students and their work has taken me away from that voice, for whole hours at a time. At the ends of days I feel too frightened and boring and repellent to go out with my friends on the staff. Instead I flee to the Adelphi Hotel.

Working in Liverpool and living in the Pennines often means nights in the Adelphi. It is the most eccentric institution, a neoclassical white monument wrapped around an interior little changed since the days of the transatlantic liners, upon which it is modelled. Waking here is like finding yourself a passenger on a ghost liner. There are great cracks in the plaster in the courtyard. Buddleia bushes sprout from the corners. The plumbing complains of the monstrous difficulty of serving hundreds of bathrooms, while the heating must burn tonnes of the national coal supply every winter day. The Victorian hope for the triumphs of future generations still hangs in the huge heart of the Adelphi's inner court, a massive space under chandeliers, its columns painted in orange-cream and white, decorated with towering glass and fanlights; it is architecture's answer to the might of the RMS *Titanic*.

Until recently there was a Father Christmas doll above the reception desk with a calendar that began on Boxing Day and counted down the days remaining until Christmas. I am sorry it is gone. It was the first sign that you had entered a peculiar world.

I am regularly the youngest guest in the place: it is a staple of pensioners' bus tours from Scotland and the North East. I chat with fellow travellers in the lifts as we drift sluggishly between floors. 'We've had a good time, but I'm glad to be going home today,' I have been told, several times. We share an affection for the prices: £33 tonight, for a cosy room, a large double with two doors, back to back, the inner covered in green leather.

Running the place is a crushing daily labour. On an afternoon last week I came across three cleaners slumped on the floor in a corner of corridors where there are no CCTV cameras, their backs to the wall.

They gave off an exhaustion you are rarely permitted to see. I recognise some of them now.

'Is it haunted?' I asked one today.

'Third and fourth are,' she said.

I am on the fourth tonight, but this room is definitely not haunted. Of the dozens of bedrooms where I have stayed, there was only one in which something felt wrong. It was a rainy, angry winter night. The room was on the top floor at the back, looking inwards. I opened the door and something in me shuddered. There was an angry draught of cold and damp and a feeling of savage dejection. I went back to reception and asked for another room.

A winter hotel, the heating always on full, the Adelphi is in its element this cold, wet night, as if far out at sea. Freezing rain slathers down in the inner courtyard. You would rather be too hot than cold at all.

My favourite Adelphi story, almost certainly apocryphal, comes via Jeff from one of his friends.

'He was checking in and a guy came down to reception and said, "I've just been mugged in the corridor on the second floor."

'The receptionist said, "Oh no. Not *again.*"'

The all-you-can-eat buffet is the heart of the hotel. Eight pounds fifty gets you a free run at a mound of food. The cabbage is good. The gravy is familiar. The roast potatoes are a reassuring yellow mush of fat. Then you must choose between battered fish which looks as though you could club a cat with it, beef like black iron turnings, a chicken leg which is too big to come from a terrestrial chicken, and the liver. I eat the liver on the grounds that a huge hit of vitamin A is probably what January needs. The slightly urinary tang does not put me off, nor the little tubes of arteries in their purple couches. I have Jenny Diski for company, *Skating to Antarctica*. My fellow diners are pallid, slow-moving, some silent but none alone. With the grand, high ceilings, where there are the moulded coats of arms of the Masons and the all-seeing eye, among other designs, and under the gaze of the white-faced waitresses, you could be in a confused dream of Eastern Europe.

A mother and her adult daughter are dining three tables away. Towards the end of the meal the mother goes slightly berserk. She has found a hair in her food. She roars and raves, shouting at the waitresses, storming out, warning anyone who speaks back to her, 'Don't go there!'

She has a local accent, as do most of the waitresses. You wonder if guest and staff all rather wish they could take the problem outside, but they are trapped in their roles. Perhaps it does not do a great deal for your sense of self-standing, to find yourself eating an eight-quid-fifty buffet of school mush at the Adelphi on a callous night in January.

In my ugly office, in the ugly building where I work, with tedious admin to service, I wonder how many office workers across the country count themselves fortunate today. At certain moments when the windows darken and the overhead light is particularly stark, there must be currents that run through all of us, to which we all feel uniquely subject, of absolute despair.

21 JANUARY

We were up throughout the middle of the night, from about three to half past four, while Aubrey summoned a series of phantom poos and asked to be told stories. We woke late from thick sleep, gummy-headed. Icy mist drifted through the trees and the woods were patched with white snow spots like freezing mould. You half expected to see a TV-documentary team pushing through the under-growth, recording the emergence and thawing of a new world. Paleoclimatologists believe ice may have covered the whole planet more than once, making a series of Snowball Earths. The retreat of the ice must have left scenes much like Hardcastle Crags this morning. Something between mist and sleet dripped out of the grey above.

Aubrey and I declared ourselves very doubtful about walking, but Rebecca is never deterred. She chivvied us into our outdoor gear and we set off for the moors above Cragg Vale. For most of the way up England's longest continual ascent you drop off into a steep valley, and rise again, up, up to Withens Clough. From the moment we parked the car everything changed. The mist thinned and wisped. There was sunlight. The surface of the reservoir was fluted with the tiniest vibrations, just enough to haze the reflections of the further banks so that the frozen moors lay sleeping on dreams of themselves. Sunlight caught in the droplets on the fence wires and I became fascinated by the rays and tiny images within them, and by the microscopic spheres of water on the stalks of mosses. Ordinary Moss, Latin name *Brachythecium rutabulum*,

is a delightful plant, like a host of tiny green diplo-
doci standing together, their heads bent heavy on
the ends of long necks, above foliage which is furred
and feathered like tiny green birds' feet.

There was proper snow here, crumping under-
foot. Just below the reservoir was a scattering of
four or five brown-white birds: snow buntings. I had
never seen them before. One sat on a tree beside the
track in good light long enough for me to be sure,
to be as sure as I could be without binoculars – yes!
I really do think so. And it was the right time and
place for them, too. They are amazing birds, able
to survive in twenty degrees below freezing. Apart
from one raven, they were the only creatures we
saw or heard. There were prints of foxes, rabbit
and a hare as we walked on. The track turned up
and over the moor into thick mist. On the edge,
as we moved into it, the air around us whitened
and thickened; you could see it condensing between
your eyes and the ground – something about the
light on the snow seemed to catch the mist in

the instants of its formation. We pressed on, circling towards Stoodley Pike, a thunderous obelisk commemorating the defeat of Napoleon, visibility down to a couple of dozen yards. And then, as we came to the lip of the land, where it falls 1,000 feet down to the Calder Valley, and the sound of a train rose from the fog far below – the miracle.

We glimpsed a burning silver disc of sun, and then quickly, so quickly, the sky paled and blued, and air absent of mist grew like lakes in the distance. Now another bluff appeared three miles away, and now another a mile beyond that, and sun and mist and the noses of the moors swam together, shoaling and clearing as if a pod of orcas were surfacing in an Arctic bay. Far to the north were lagoons of pure turquoise. We seemed to gaze on islands and inlets of sea, and a black-bellied cloud, and then blue nearer us, and the snow shone in the sun. There was a wonderful lifting in the sight of it, like the granting of a brief rest. I felt like a prisoner on day release.

At Stoodley Pike we turned away from the valley and took a track across the moor towards thick conifer woods. The path through them was wild going, bog and marsh, snow and mud, tussocked and threatening to suck us down. Aubrey rode on my shoulders, sharing my enthusiasm for a real adventure, and we talked of shaggy St Bernards rescuing benighted alpinists. On the further side we forged through marsh, bracken, bog and snow, Aubrey stalwart now and the terrain properly rough. It must have been like riding a drunken camel. We caught sight of the car and cheered.

'I'm not coming back up here until the summer,' Aubrey declared. Earlier, when we tried to persuade him to walk rather than be carried, the better to warm his poor feet, he said, 'I'm not falling for your devious tricks!'

25 JANUARY

The pre-dawn darkness presses over Hebden Bridge, where two elderly men are taking coffee in the station café.

'You're even more antisocial than me,' says one, 'and I'm bloody antisocial.'

'I don't like people.'

'I don't like 'em either.'

'I don't even like animals.'

'I don't like dogs.'

26 JANUARY

Day breaks over Liverpool in the delighted crying of herring gulls as they turn in a towering blue morning, cold and clear. The pipes of the Adelphi stream steam. You see bright day-fires like this in New York, in London, in Marrakech: these are mornings for cities rising to the day, and every spirit is lifted.

My archetype of a winter city morning came in Saint Étienne, in the southern Massif of France. I had moved abroad for the first time, coming south on the train from Paris to teach English in a *lycée*. On the first night I drank with my new flatmates; one, Robert, a much older American, read Paul Valéry and Rimbaud and poured whisky until suddenly the walls tilted and the floor changed shape. At eighteen I knew nothing of hangovers and almost nothing of France. Waking to both was exquisite. Outside was a freezing blue brightness, and sunlight that seemed too raw for heat or colour, while through the flat, very quietly, ran a rill of music I had never heard before. 'In my mind I'm going to Carolina,' James Taylor sang. The hangover was no pain. It slowed time and heightened senses. Taylor's voice, his slow melody, seemed to tune the whole day. The moment fell into that strange place of consciousness in which you are aware that what you are experiencing is being laid down like a tile in the mosaic of memory, to last as long as the mind. Everything was new: the black coffee hissing on the gas flame, the smell of baking outside, the sigh and moan of the trams. We went out into the Place Jean Jaurès. The cold was intense, as if the icy blue had taken form and texture.

'Ça kai,' Robert said. He hesitated; he had an American reserve about swearing. 'It means . . . fuckin' freezing.'

'Ça kai,' I repeated, relishing authentic French slang. 'Ça kai!'

I gave it like a salute to the arches of the Hôtel de Ville, to the unfinished tower of the St Charles Cathedral, to the new frigid air of France.

That winter was the first of my adult life. We lived on little, experimenting with pasta tossed in raw egg, with turning packet soup into sauce and all the permutations of rice and tins. When we were paid by the schools where we taught we gorged on sumptuous kebabs, thick half-moons of bread stuffed with dripping lamb, *sauce piquante* and *sauce blanche*, and chocolate and banana crêpes from kiosks. We learned to make cassoulet out of fat and cabbage.

On frosty Saturdays I circled and criss-crossed the city. In the darkness before dawn one Sunday morning I took buses into the Massif to watch the sun rise over the snowfields and the city waking in the distance; to watch the play of light on the traffic, the steam of factories, the slide and sidle of trains and trams and the first flights overhead from Lyon. It was the strangest sensation – that moment of disbelief which comes with the twitch of comprehension at all the lives, the impossible myriad million deeds down there, taking place in an instant, in inconceivable profusion, and yet for a second the mind seems to glimpse the scale and variety of them, as if you look into the distant future or the far past and can actually see . . . It was never there, perhaps, but for the sensation of having glimpsed, which remains.

Such days die like gilded embers, glowing down. In the twilight on the train back across the flat-lands towards Manchester, two ladies are discussing death and disease.

'I was pregnant with Tom when I lost his father. Now Pauline's got Alzheimer's . . . she went down as soon as she lost him.'

'They do,' says the other, 'they do.'

To live with the weather, the damp and the dark-ness demands and imparts solidarity, strengthens friendship and families. If you look on the dimmer side of anything you are lost. When Uncle Chris turned the car over, his mother transformed the event into a triumph of luck.

'Nobody was hurt,' Jenny said, 'that's what I'm telling myself, and thank goodness.'

I hope I am becoming better at thanking good-ness. It comes naturally in the summer, in happiness, in beauty. I look up and say, 'Thank you — *thank you!*' in a passionate whisper. But it is easy to thank goodness then.

In the winter you need strategies. I know of many, anecdotally. Among my friends are devotees of Bikram yoga, light boxes and counselling. Some dedicate themselves to cooking, cold-water swimming or medication. Northern Man knows how it is done in the dark time. I see him coming in a bobble of small, blazing lights. Down through the wood the white stars cascade and buckle, then with a whizzing sound the pack approaches. Now their voices well up in a deep, rooky cawing of Yorkshire accents. The mountain bikers are travelling in a conversation, as if the woods and the valley gloom are as snug as a pub. They are spattered in mud and sluiced in rain, their faces flushed with oxygen and bushed with beards.

'Oh 'ee did yeah – an' ah told 'im 'ee would!'

'Ee's a one for it though, you've got to give it to 'im.'

And they're gone. I admire it hugely, that thrust and determination. They will set out in anything, the worse the better. They batter the weather back, pump up the hills and smash down the valleys. They baste the moors with their tracks and lash the twigs with their faces; they wear the mud like medals.

27 JANUARY

A mist day, a moss day, a day of rain that never quite fell. In the woods Aubrey and his friend Alex hurled themselves up banks, conquered rocks, swung on branches, danced and dived down mud heaps. They are impervious to this drear grey shroud.

No birds moved and few called, only the moss and the fungi seemed alive, though there were green spears where the narcissi were rising and the first snowdrops came out yesterday. Where the beck torrents through rapids it made a scarf of mist which floated over that one spot, a spectre. Later, in a twilit instant, there came a rushing roar over the valley, the Buttress trees bowed and shook and clouds tore themselves apart, a pale sky promising stars behind them. A blackbird and a robin sang as the light failed. There was a wild flaring of pinks and oranges in flaying streamers of high cloud as the moon rose, waxing. Now there were two skies, one flying low and fast, small gigs and racing skiffs of cloud, while higher contrails crossed white paths and barely drifted. We have heard no owls for weeks but Rebecca saw one out the back, perched on the fence. There are mice around the water outflow in the garden; the tawny owl was in ambush, waiting.

In the moments when I am watching, recording or sharing these things with Aubrey or Rebecca, I am well. It is in the gaps between that the panic comes. Unable to do much beyond self-loathe, I dedicate myself to simple tasks. Brushing the carpet, taking out the recycling, hoovering, washing, drying, sorting and putting away clothes: for weeks I feel like a live-in domestic help, backing up Rebecca as she works.

29 JANUARY

Money worries, taxes, troubles. I have spent and not saved, and now I must scrabble for cash, cut all spending, and work out a way out of debt. And somehow I must not let the worry make me a terrible father and a ghastly person to live with. I will fail at this – I am failing at this, I know. The negative, like an egg hatching, produces a kind of dark thing which sits in my mouth, spitting out gloom whenever it can. I try not to speak.

With Aubrey I pretend to be someone else, someone unworried, balanced and loving. It feels like a rotten impersonation, but the little boy is so forgiving and encouraging. He counted to 100, and he played Snakes and Ladders beautifully, beating me with style and accuracy. Then he invented his own version, where you dodge around snakes and take running jumps at the ladders. I ran on the spot, my legs running away with me, sideways and back, while he laughed and clapped. Rebecca danced to Mariachi music in the kitchen, delighting him. We are no model family, but we have life. Winter suits this house, with the fire going, the clothes hanging on the drying rack, the door curtain pulled across and the key turned in the lock, a fractional attempt to stem the freezing draught from the keyhole.

Going up and down the valley today there were lovely, turning clouds in the blue, the high moor showing yellow, red and drained green under the sun. It looked like a plate from the Shell Guides, those visions of the British countryside rich in colour and nature. We lack much in West Yorkshire, but we do not quite lack that. It lifted me. The nights have been much more beautiful than the days for a while now. Beck-rush and moonlight, pale patinas of ghost cloud, and behind them the stars, tiny, red and blue and white.

1 FEBRUARY

The valley is a river of light before dawn, the super blue blood moon a silver-white portal, flooding the air with luminous cold. There is black ice on the road and the fields have a glow about them as day-break to the south-east sends light like a tidal flow to meet the moon's fading downpour.

2 FEBRUARY

Friday-evening trains from Manchester Victoria into the Pennines are a triumph of human spirit. We board the usual old thing, a tattered and achy sort of train which has had many owners, currently the German state railway company Deutsche Bahn, via

Arriva, via Northern: a poor train for poor people, they all conclude. The passengers board it gently, careful with each other, sweetly polite. We bear slowly east into the dusk. Three girls are budgeting. They are Rochdalians.

'We don't have to have the fizzy drinks.'

'How much would that bring it down to?'

'Under twenty.'

'How much under?'

'How much did we spend already?'

'Less than ten.'

'There you are then. We don't need it. I like water!'

The first speaker will be a doctor, I think; the way she watches the other two and sways them; her look is quick, her interventions light and decisive. The girls are Muslims, clear-eyed, respectful, their voices confident. You want to hug the parents of these children who understand the world so well.

Guidance for Muslims in winter is touching in its absolute practicality. Columnists from Islamic

Help, citing hadiths, refer to the cold as 'an enemy that enters quickly but leaves slowly'. Wear woollen layers (the Prophet Muhammad was a great fan of wool: 'grazing livestock He has created for you, in them is warmth', says the Koran), cover your head and wrap up, 'even if going out to put the bins out perhaps, or to get something out of the car; a few moments of being exposed to the cold is enough to make a person ill'.

The mix of common sense and hyperbole makes a fine portrait of a practical faith; advice that comes down from the desert nights of the seventh century applies equally to the streets of Lancashire.

The season binds us across time and place. In illustrated manuscripts the calendar pages which preface psalters and books of hours show this. Near Bruges in February around 1500, men in hats and boots cut wood with billhooks while a woman in red gathers the sticks behind them. In France two centuries earlier, a man in a tunic, cloak and hood holds a wet shoe to dry near a blazing fire. The refrain for rich men was sitting as close to the fire as possible, eating as much as possible and having women bring food to the table, according to fourteenth-century manuscripts from Bruges and Ghent.

Earlier still, the Venerable Bede's *De temporum ratione*, The Reckoning of Time, written in the eighth century, is our source for the pre-Roman calendar. Winter began in October, the month of *Winterfylleth*, the winter full moon. November, *Blotmonath*, was the month of blood sacrifice. Our sheep lying slaughtered in the field were killed on the cusp of this time. December, *Aerra Geola*, was the month before Yule, and January, *Aefterra Geola*, the month after. February was *Solmonath*, from *sol*, wet mud or sand. What the Romans saw as Mars' time, the fighting season, the Anglo-Saxons named for a fertility goddess, Rheda, and April for Eostre, a goddess of the dawn and the equinox, whose name is a mother of Easter. As Bede reckoned time, so his time reckoned him: as an Anglo-Saxon your age was counted in winters.

Over the western plain the sky was clear; as we approached Manchester we came under a dark bar of cloud. Now, as we close with the fingers of the moors, the windows of the foothill towns are lighting and there is a peace in the gloaming valleys, a drawing-in as the earth turns us and night comes down from the wild tops as if drawn to the warmth of our settlements.

3 FEBRUARY

Saturday morning, hustings in Halifax, and Rebecca is going to vote. Aubrey and I will take her. It is a winter morning of cruel hostility, sleet falling, the sky grown grey and cold to overflowing. We drop Rebecca at Halifax Minster, a bony and beautiful fifteenth-century church which looks as though the cold and rain have charred it black. Its tower proclaims a certainty of God against all siege. (I have been to Halifax a dozen times and never seen the sun here.) Aubrey likes the sound of the Calderdale Industrial Museum.

'We're slightly overstaffed!' says one volunteer, as two of them hand us our visitor badges, in case, she says, there is a fire.

They are wonderfully overstaffed. About thirty retirees garrison the rooms.

We are lectured on lathes and drills, on diesel and steam, on coal mines and looms, on sweet-wrapping machines and worsted.

The looms are astounding time machines of stretched thread.

'You see that man in the photograph there?' says a small, round man with an enormous voice. In a black-and-white picture, a loom like a series of houses of thread dwarfs the tiny figure who stands framed in it. 'That was my dad! And he told me I were going to be a loom-tuner, and I was.'

We play I-spy as the hustings voters come in. Rebecca arrives; she has made friends and cast votes and we want to know who and for what and why. She is glowing with the engagement and the issues, the speeches and the battle. 'One of them said they wanted to support mothers over education. What about fathers!'

Back through the rain and gloom we go, undaunted. There are winter days like this that seem to set out to break you, thick cloud and the horizons grime-grey, sludging into dirty brown, when windscreen spray and wipers have no effect on the view. You think the glass must be filthy, but no, a murky, heavy oppression lowers from the clouds, permeating the horizons. Instead we bobble and battle along. We take on the bedroom and the house, clearing, cleaning and sorting. Aubrey makes a tableau of dinosaurs eating farm-ers. It is extremely vivid.

7 FEBRUARY

It snowed almost tenderly all day yesterday, from first light until the afternoon began to wane into twilight. A few degrees warmer and we would have been in thick mist, not rain – snow crystals form from water in its gaseous, not its liquid state. There was a persistence and a stillness in the air, even as the flakes fell. The smell in the valley was a bare tang, exhilarating. The salt-gritter driver paused for a word, a man with a black hat and a ruddy round face, twinkling as if he played the lead in a salt-gritting film. 'It's all the time at the moment,' he said. 'You just can't tell. Yorkshire!'

And then the snow stopped and the twilight was beautiful, all the valley's contours, the earth, dimly sugared, foregrounding the woods. The trees' tangle of cross-branches appeared especially bright, their verticals pale gold or faint purple. A blue tit launched the same three notes from the top of a hazel – the energy it must take for song from such a small body! And a pheasant crowed; they have been quiet for a while now, though this was the summer of the pheasants, crocking and thrumming.

Today was the one shatteringly clear day so far. The sky glowed from pure, cold dark to a dim luminous lapis to a bright glaze-blue. Sunlight flared up the valley, catching the pines on the Buttress. Not a drop of moisture in the air anywhere, the land wonderfully clenched and clipped in the frost. At night the first tawny owl I have heard for weeks, a male, yipping. The gritting lorries patrol like battleships.

This diary is a refuge, a thing to do, something to put work and time into, a defence against the hopelessness. This depression is a terrible disabler. You cannot flow from one thing that needs to be done to the next; you constantly pause and doubt and disbelieve. When I do the shopping I make a list and stick to it, as if incapable of improvising.

'Is this all?' I ask Rebecca, before I go. 'Is this really everything we need? I'm really struggling with cognitive functioning,' I confess. 'You must have noticed.'

'Of course,' she says, patiently.

Aubrey is going to think that all his father ever did or could do was the washing-up.

For lectures I find myself writing down every word I will deliver; in conversations I can hardly hear what the other person is saying, so busy is my brain in discarding possible responses, judging them all inadequate or inappropriate. Thank goodness for my students. They seem to sense my vulnerability, and my anxiety on their behalf. I am running a new course for them, in non-fiction, and they have taken to it in a wonderful, engaged way. Many suffer anxiety and depression and self-doubt, but they have not been asked to write about themselves before at university, and they are finding relief in it. They write with restraint and clarity and no self-pity at all about absent fathers, eating disorders, periods of homelessness, and about shame – shame produced by a belief that they will never make the money their parents did, and are therefore guilty of failing to justify the privileges of happy homes and good schools. Their writing is often heartbreaking to read. They write about routine bullying and humiliation at work: the way shoppers treat them as they stack shelves, make coffee, sell shoes – the relentless pressure from managers to sell more shoes, to persuade customers to 'take advantage' of special offers. The girls record sexual harassment, leering, groping. Some students, halfway or two-thirds of the way through their degrees, hugely in debt, seeing no future as writers or anything else, suffer breakdowns, withdrawals, depressions, relentless anxiety and sleep disorders. We refer them to student support, to counselling; a number of times I have walked someone to the counsellors, both of us knowing that they will not manage more than one appointment, that they do not believe their troubles can be fixed by talking.

Without some shard of belief, without a degree of hope, there is no system that can help them. I recognise the condition. How dare anyone call them snowflakes – they are mighty. The pressures they face are unprecedented, their prospects of stimulating, rewarding, validating work seem tenuous at best: how will they compete against an automated future, in which the fortunate few will earn millions, and millions will be dismissed as unfortunate?

At the day's end you long to unload the anger and indignation, but I cannot inflict myself on my friends. I pine for them. I wish I could go out and make my colleagues Jeff and Demelza laugh and hear their stories, and live life as it should be lived, in conversation and joy and interest, always in interest. But there is no way. If I open my mouth all that will come out will be glum blue guilt. No one should have to hear it.

9 FEBRUARY

Like the Great Gatsby in Rochdale, Gin Night came to the town hall. I had not drunk for two weeks, but we were committed – they were raising money for the Cricket Club, which is sacred, and Cousin Matthew's birthday was coming: the clan gathered. And I wanted to see inside this famous building, which Rochdalians believe was beloved by Hitler and destined to be transported to Germany and rebuilt there in the event of Nazi victory. It is a thunderous mass of Gothic Revival, portly, stately and oddly elegant, with a clock tower that does look as though it hankers to be beside the Rhine.

Under a painting of the signing of the Magna Carta – King John looking a bit wispy under his golden crown, facing a baron dressed for a crusade – with carved black angels like ships' figureheads flying above us, Rochdale society gathered to taste, wince or grin, laugh, taste again, comment and gossip. Lancashire came out to play, smart in wide belts, suits, bright ski jackets, short dresses. Every size and shape of body was in the room, the icy night magnificently disregarded. We were thin, we were lumpy-plump, we were buff, we were red-faced, we were elegant. The singer was flat-capped in tweeds and waistcoat. Two elderly couples took turns to dance the Charleston on the stage beneath the organ pipes. One of the men, ebulliently moustached, was particularly good. I congratulated him.

'Tell the organisers!' he cried. 'They'll book me again!'

Rebecca's brother Chris, sister Emma, cousin Matthew and Auntie Jen were there. Matthew is the most powerful speaker. He fixes you from height with a dark eye and confides boomingly.

'Me dad's second marriage, and me mum's second marriage, both in here. There's a theme there. To us, Rochdale town centre was amazing when we were young. Where Asda is now? That was the Cricket before they moved it. Round behind Tesco was the Woolworths Working Men's Club.

The Club's still there. The Regal Moon used to be a cinema. They'd have queues around the block on weekends. And I tell you what, it looks a lot better now than it has for years. The new council building has won awards – have you seen the way the river sweeps by it? Rochdale was wonderful to us, you know, before you get older and look around . . .'

The men's voices are bass rolls, flattened and warmed with the Lancashire burr.

'Coom on! Give uz a fiver! Coom on, fiver each!' blasted a big, bluff man with a carrier bag full of raffle tickets. An elfin man in a smart suit joined us; he wore a sweet smile like a disguise.

'Who is he?' I asked, when he went to replenish his gin.

'That's Danny! Danny Callaghan.'

'His mum is the most amazing woman I have ever met,' Rebecca said.

'She had seven of them,' Emma put in. 'Seven! And they all look just like Danny.'

'They're like Russian dolls,' Auntie Jen giggled.

'Oh she was so fierce!' Rebecca said. 'Absolutely ferocious.'

'She had to be. They were properly naughty boys.'

'She's only about four feet high.'

'And they're all lovely.'

'So tiny and so fierce! When one of them had his birthday she put huge banners out on the main road.'

The marble busts of Victorian Members of Parliament surveyed their descendants and inheritors as we flowed up and down the grand staircase, and back and forth under the fan vaulting of the vestibule. In the Great Hall, under the hammer beams, I thought of the Venerable Bede's eighth-century report of the nature of existence as perceived and explained by a kinsman to the Christian King Eorpwald of East Anglia:

The present life of man upon earth, O King, seems to me in comparison with that time which is unknown to us like the swift flight of a sparrow through the mead-hall where you sit at supper in winter, with your Ealdormen and thanes, while the fire blazes in the midst and the hall is warmed, but the wintry storms of rain or snow are raging abroad. The sparrow, flying in at one door and immediately out at another, whilst he is within, is safe from the wintry tempest, but after a short space of fair weather, he immediately vanishes out of your sight, passing from winter to winter again. So this life of man appears for a little while, but of what is to follow or what went before we know nothing at all.

We are a great many mighty sparrows, chattering up the warm hall. We are managers in floral shirts, teachers with blue hair, distributors in conker leather (the North wears the best shoes in England), contractors in short skirts, rosy technicians who run marathons, traders neatly tucked in, retired academics in best grey woollen jackets, council officers in gleaming specs, logistics planners dressed as if for church, estate agents with bustle, police officers invisibly uniformed. We are jacketed and high-heeled restaurateurs. We are smart and chattering, gaudy and bellowsome, big-boned and roving, quick-eyed and balding, fond of our food and fountains of drinking stories, raised on black peas, black pudding, black stone and ball games, car-proud, dog-loving, grit-grin-and-give-a-hug, say-it-as-we-see-it and who's next to the bar? We are Rochdale on a mead-hall night.

It is not so much the philosophy in Bede's account which speaks, as I mill with the crowd, but the account of Anglo-Saxon winter: tempest, rain and snow, and all at once, no doubt. The week has been hard; the weekend will bring sleet and more rain, and tempest tomorrow night, but, as Matthew said, the beams are beautiful, and lamps hanging from them are beautiful; under their tallow-yellow light the loyalty and solidarity in the room is a palpable thing.

Outside it was bitter. Youths yawed and reeled in front of the Regal Moon. The cheapest taxis in Britain queued outside, the drivers, Muslim and teetotal, readying themselves for the breath of their passengers. On the icy drive home a boy fell into the road in Todmorden. He was dragged off it by his friends, reeling and helpless. A police van lurked behind the supermarket; Rebecca spotted it and had me turn around.

'We'd want someone to do it if it was Robin,' she said.

Beside the driver, a tank of a man with a skull like a granite egg, his partner officer looked very young and scared. Todmorden must be a tough beat on a winter Friday; teenagers scattered along the tight pavements, wild between booze and cold.

Above the valley the stars were blue and green and white. The salt grit lay in pink mats on the roads. A single tawny owl called from the other side of the river then fell silent, listening as the valley listened.

10 FEBRUARY

A vile, violently cold day with nothing in the world to recommend it, I thought, having woken before dawn and gone up to the attic, watching the sky turn from dark to indigo to wet slate as sleet fell on the skylights, filling them slowly.

We breakfasted on porridge, as have the people of Europe since the Paleolithic, according to researchers in Italy, who analysed a nomad's grinding stone from 32,000 years ago and found oats, though our ancestors would have struggled to boil it until the invention of pottery in the late Pleistocene

12,000 years ago. Their wild oats, heated, ground and cooked with hot water, would not have tasted so different from our winter diet. Porridge has been a staple around the world ever since, the sweet, esculent smell of it and the green and gold syrup tins an unchanged link between the kitchens of parents and children now.

'Stodgy,' Aubrey declared.

'But with lashings of honey!' I countered.

Afterwards he drew a huge green man being struck by lightning, then rehearsed his letters, writing his name. We curled on the sofa and read old books, for the comfort and the spelling, and did jigsaws and discussed what would happen if half the house was under water and there was a killer whale downstairs. He loves killer whales. In the evening Rebecca went out and Aubrey requested the Labours of Heracles. His favourites are the Augean stables, the slaying of the Hydra and Heracles tricking Atlas into taking back the sky. When it is time to sleep he rolls over and I send him off, sometimes with another reading, given as a soft drone. He was gone before I had done two lines of Jan Morris on Venice, which is my winter city.

Rebecca and I came to know Venice very well in the years we lived in Verona, but the first time I saw the city my brother and I were young enough to share a room with our mother, who decided we should take advantage of a windfall and a Christmas package at the Hotel Ala: three stars and breakfast included.

'We'll fill up on breakfast and we'll eat supper somewhere cheap,' she declared, and so we went. There were very few tourists. I recognised the same couples crossing the bridges and the same faces in the squares. Filling up on breakfast was sweet work: croissants they called *cornetti* stuffed with apricot jam, fuel for expeditions to the churches and galleries. At nightfall we returned to the same restaurant, which asked few lire, less when they knew us, for polenta and liver. I was old enough to be turned loose to range along the canals and quays, becoming lost for hours. On Christmas Eve we went to midnight Mass in St Mark's, a great gold Byzantine barn, dim-shadowed, gilded, towering, a planet filled to the base of the columns with Venetians.

Rambling families, the grandparents in furs and the babies in hats, made a tide of the city's people which filled the naves, spilled into the transepts and lapped up against the pillars. Adults talked and children ate snacks as the Italian and Latin and incense drifted over us. I had never seen religion so informal and so inhabited. In this God's house you could eat and talk as the Patriarch led the prayers, conducting a service to which you brought rugs for your knees, in a cavern like a heaven, with the angels, the saints and the evangelists shimmering over you in glass gold tesserae. It seemed the point was not to follow the words but to be present at their incantation. As I gazed into the apses and arches the whole basilica turned upside down. We hung suspended over deep, gleaming pools where the figures of the archangels, St John the Baptist, St Peter, St Isadore and St Mark himself shone in mosaics of shadow, gold-glint and holy dark.

Venice in winter! Furious bursts of sleet scour out the alleys, driving you wet-footed into cafés, tight and warm as the cells of a beehive. The fog makes a second sea over the lagoon where the vaporetti, the water buses, manoeuvre like baleens, feeling through the murk by sound and echo. Winter thins down the visitor tide. The rumble of suitcase wheels diminishes. In the Frari, Titian's Virgin ascends in scarlet and sunfire to the solo of a lone chorister. Bitter dawns bring seagulls to dispute with cats over the rubbish sacks as the boatmen blow into their scarves and chafe. Winter makes the ochres and yellows of the Riva degli Schiavoni a pastel scale running up to the flourish of the Doge's Palace, pink as seashell, white-boned and fluted, its feet in the water come *acqua-alta*, the flood tide.

The first time Rebecca saw the city she burst into tears at the beauty of it. We went often, taking cheap train rides from Verona, and walked it in the hours and days most visitors shun. In winter the play of light and cold gives a hardness and precision to the city's shades and suggestions. Joseph Brodsky caught it wonderfully in *Watermark*, his meditation on the city in winter. He was so fond of Venice in this season that he vowed never to visit in summer: 'In the morning this light breasts your windowpane and, having pried your eye open like a shell, runs ahead of you, strumming its lengthy rays – like a hot-footed schoolboy running his stick along the iron grate of a park or garden – along arcades, colonnades, red-brick chimneys, saints, and lions.' 'The espresso at your cup's bottom is the only small black dot in, you feel, a miles-long radius,' he wrote.

Venice froze repeatedly in the eighteenth century, in 1709, 1789 and 1791. In the first, Europe's worst winter for 500 years, a Venetian senator, Pietro Garzoni, described all the canals and the lagoon as 'petrified by cold'. Boats transporting food and wood were cut through the ice by work-men from the city's fortress, the Arsenale, with pickaxes. The Duchess of Orléans, shivering in front of a fire at Versailles despite being wrapped in furs, reported wine freezing in bottles and informed her correspondent that she struggled to hold her pen. Church bells shattered, trees fractured and it was possible to walk across the Baltic from Denmark to Sweden. A Swedish attack on Russia during the Great Northern War collapsed when 2,000 troops died of cold in a single night.

Descriptions from 1789 are even more vivid, thanks to the diaries of Giuseppe Gennari: 'Sudden ice crusts form on the running stream, and the water bears on its surface iron-bound wheels – once welcoming ships, but now to broad wagons! Everywhere brass splits, clothes freeze on the back, and they cleave with axes the liquid wine; whole lakes turn into a solid mass, and the rough icicle hardens on the unkempt beard.'

Gennari sounds excited and energised by the cold and drama. Goodness knows what he would have made of the North of England. Here rain falls, tyres slush and mould grows in bathrooms. The other side of living with nature, which blesses us so much in the summer, is its bullying ever-presence now. It is different in the South. Living in London, working in Broadcasting House, dashing from office to home, or office to bar or restaurant or theatre or cinema and home, I barely noticed the weather. Darkness outside the office windows before four o'clock: so what? Water running down the steps at the entrance to Oxford Circus, so what? Nature in the city was a mere inconvenience: umbrellas, tubes delayed by flooding, buses packed with steaming shoulders. I saw ten London winters in and out. None of them had a tenth of the power of a Pennine week in January.

11 FEBRUARY

A ferocious day of sleet and snow, flickers of sun, then hail, sleet and more snow. We have done a winter shop for half-term, laying in supplies. The kitchen is a pile of stores. Robin, keen to take advantage of his holiday, lies in bed, repelling our attempts to shift him to productivity. Peeling potatoes, washing-up, washing and drying, putting out the compost, making the beds, writing practice and alphabet jigsaws with Aubrey: the scene here is not unlike a winter day in 1834 at the Parsonage at Haworth, just over the moor. A famous account is signed by Emily and Anne Brontë, then sixteen and fourteen, but written by Emily. It is cherished for its insight into the extraordinary life of the Parsonage, which is now a museum:

I fed Rainbow, Diamond Snowflake Jasper pheasant (alias) this morning Branwell went down to Mr Driver's and brought news that

Sir Robert Peel was going to be invited to stand for Leeds Anne and I have been peeling apples for Charlotte to make us an apple pudding and for Aunt nuts and apples Charlotte said she made puddings perfectly and she was of a quick but limited intellect. Taby said just now Come Anne pilloputate (i.e. pill a potato) Aunt has come into the kitchen just now and said where are your feet Anne Anne answered On the floor Aunt papa opened the parlour door and gave Branwell a letter saying here Branwell read this and show it to your Aunt and Charlotte – The Gondals are discovering the interior of Gaaldine Sally Mosley is washing in the back kitchen

It is past Twelve o'clock Anne and I have not tidied ourselves, done our bedwork or done our lessons and we want to go out to play we are going to have for Dinner Boiled Beef, Turnips, potatoes and applepudding. The Kitchin is in a very untidy state Anne and I have not done our music exercise which consists of b major Taby said on my putting a pen in her face Ya pitter pottering there instead of pilling a potate I answered O Dear, O Dear, O dear I will directly with that I get up, take a knife and begin pilling (finished) pilling the potatoes papa going to walk Mr Sunderland expected.

Our equivalent of Gondal, the imaginary country created by Emily and Anne, is the continent where live Aubrey's dinosaurs, venomous snakes, killer whales and storm troopers. Josh Fenton-Glynn, the Labour candidate who won the hustings, is our Robert Peel. Robin and I have had the 'ya pitter pottering (on the internet) instead of helping' conversation many times.

The intermingling of many lives in restricted space is one of the wonders of the Parsonage. The dining room, where the sisters wrote, is exquisite. It was their habit to pace around the table, discussing their stories. They must have moved like dancers, feet falling precisely in measured steps as they debated. Our house is a narrow vessel, anchored in this inlet in the moors. The front room can be paced, but the rest is small, full, wooden and creaky. I give thanks for it, daily. I dreamed of bailiffs last night, chasing me through barns.

12 FEBRUARY

Aubrey's first day at his new school! He is starting mid-term, but he was hungry to make the change. His kindergarten has run its time, we all felt.

'I am so bored of going on walks,' he had announced. 'I want to go to reading school.' This accords with Rebecca's philosophy of reading when readiness strikes, and suddenly he has a school uniform, a book bag, a class and two teachers, Miss Hannan and Mrs Beevers, both of whom seem excellent: Miss Hannan is pale from winter and work; Mrs Beevers has an indestructible look. Aubrey has friends there already, and the school is accustomed to taking children in transition from Steiner.

There was thick snow this morning as we set off. The children looked magnificent, boys pelting snowballs, girls marching to their classes, the Headmistress buttering toast (the person who normally feeds the breakfast club had not made it) and little Aubrey feeling all our nerves. He was so stalwart! He looked glad we were going, actually; let me get on with it, his face said. When we collected him at three he appeared, poking his tongue out, and dashed gleefully around the playground with Robin. He ate every mouthful of his supper without any prompting. He seemed quite transformed.

This winter is taking a lot out of us, as a family. We are living tightly, Rebecca swaying between unbelievable patience and sudden tempers, me trapped between self-imprisoned fear, disbelieving self-disgust and tentative moments of optimism, and both of us trying not to let the boys be affected by our troubles. But we are gathering, too. Tonight we played cards in front of the fire, and Robin managed to leave his phone alone, and we laughed, and it was truly lovely. Progress! Hope! Robin said it was 'just like old times'. In Rochdale before we emigrated, in Italy and on our travels we have always played cards and laughed. Robin was a brilliant child who has turned into a sweet young man. He's a right bugger to get out of bed in the mornings, of course, but we have come to an unspoken agreement for the period between his waking and his train to school. We say very little and try to be civil.

'Morning Rob.'

'Morning Horace.'

'Got everything?'

'Yep.'

'Let's go . . .'

15 FEBRUARY

Wake in the early hours to spats of hail-rain on the skylight and an ominous thump from the mattress beside me. And another: a leak in the roof. Oh hell, oh hell. Now what? We've only had it break through once before, during the Boxing Day floods, when the volume of water coming down was diabolical. Fold towel, catch drips, go back to sleep. No sleep. Slowly dawn comes, hovering back, the frost so hard the ground looks creamy. Slowly comes the blue, a longing, soaring blue, crisp as glass. The sheep in the meadow by the stream are frosted into place. Their trick is not to move at all, to let the crystals cover them, and so they blanket themselves to the earth.

My mornings follow a pattern, beginning around three or four, when I jolt awake, absolutely alert, suddenly. I put the pillow over my head and try to return to sleep, but it will not have me. I turn and turn over worry and grim visions as if on a slow spit. At six or seven when the alarm goes I surface, guilty and exhausted. I dress, wash, go downstairs, forget things — I forget things all the time — go back up, change clothes (I cannot make decisions, have no confidence in any choice), go down again. If I do not smoke I will be hopping with self-loathing and irritation. I will be short with Aubrey when he delays breaking away from his Lego, or refuses to eat his breakfast or resists doing his teeth. To drain the irritation I smoke, and the guilt of smoking floods in with the relief of the nicotine. I resolve not to smoke again, and simultaneously despise myself for the emptiness of the resolution, stand in the rain and roar with incredulity that this is my existence, and with fury at myself, for it is only my fault.

16 FEBRUARY

Last night was deep winter, freezing starlight over the valley and Rebecca warming the whole house as she banked up the fire. I looked at her and loved her and felt I had let her down so utterly, not saving enough, not planning enough, not loving and cherishing enough, worrying too much, changing too little, being away too much.

It is hard to describe someone you know so well, as hard as attempting a vivid travel piece about your home town. I thought I must write a book about Rebecca as I came to know her, a portrait of the girl she described and how she became the woman who seemed made to be the heroine of a story, whom I met when I walked into one of the worst hotels in Marrakech and took the only free seat in the lobby.

Opposite was a laughing, tall, beautiful figure with what I thought in that moment were auburn hair and green eyes. Actually, her eyes are deep bright blue and her hair brown.

Moments earlier she had been asked by her friend what sort of man she wished to meet – she was separated from her husband – and said, 'Someone who finds that Christmas decoration up there as funny as I do.' (The scrumple of tinsel was in a far corner of the ceiling, in a Muslim hotel, in March.) A writer, she said, or a South African sailor.

I was on my way from South Africa to Wales, writing about following swallows.

But how to describe Rebecca . . .

She is deeply, naturally, faithful, but she seems to inspire feelings as strong as jealousy. One of her ex-boyfriends cut all her clothes in half, scissoring a line through the middle of them as they hung in a wardrobe. Another burned her clothes and chopped up the wardrobe in which she kept them – a lovely wardrobe, she said, that had belonged to her granny. She dumped another – they are still friends – after he presented her with a list of everything she spent and what it went on. She had punched him for making a pass at her sister.

'In the middle of the face, as hard as you can,' she says is the way to punch a man, because you may only get one chance. She is a pacifist, or at least violently anti-war.

She walks and sits with a very straight back, a legacy of following a love of Tai Chi to Taiwan where her instructor was an elderly lady Tai Chi Master.

'I wanted to learn the sword, but she said, "You cannot learn the sword if you are pregnant." I didn't know I was.'

'She's so . . . *righteous*!' my friend Nathan exclaimed, after meeting her. She is certainly highly moral. You rarely meet anyone so unfamiliar with grey areas or compromise.

She loves widely, hugely; it is how she lives. Life-changer, life-enhancer. She is slightly somehow *other* . . . my nicknames for her include Fairy, Elf and Goblin, in tribute to a pagan spirituality which seems to attend her, as if naturally, unsolicited, and to a sense of difference about her, as though she is of a slightly variant species.

She has high, Slavic cheek bones, her eyes set now in tiny curving laughter lines. It was thought there was something wrong with her when she was a baby, when those eyes seemed not to focus.

'She didn't say anything for years,' her father said. 'Then one day she sort of shook herself, opened her mouth and started talking. She hasn't stopped since.'

'I was away with the fairies,' she says.

One of her great-grandmothers was known as The Witch. Her father sometimes calls her that, laughing.

In the middle of the night she sleeps on her back, her arms flung out, and she seems to go somewhere utterly far away, out across a wide deep sea. It is as if some home, some otherwhere, is reclaiming her. For the boys and me she is our captain, our heroine, our champion, our audience and greatest friend.

The rain came gently this morning, not hard enough to penetrate the roof, thank goodness. I have no solution to the leak but prayer and pushing the slates back. Two of them went a little way in; we'll see. The wall at the top of the garden has collapsed. Mighty hewed blocks of millstone grit, they must have taken three strong men each, over a century ago. Winter of wreckage! If the Revenue declares me bankrupt, if the bailiffs come, if we have to sell the house . . . On the table was Aubrey's certificate from his first assembly: he was Star of the Week, honoured for settling in so beautifully.

Slept with a clench in my gut.

17 FEBRUARY

And then a new day, blue and hopeful. Frieda the dog and I set out for the obelisk on a bluff above the wood. A thin squirrel scratted up a beech tree and there were birds moving everywhere, blue tits, great tits, blackbirds, and, when we reached the top, a buzzard. A couple stood on the path, paused in the wood.

'A lovely day at last!' said he.

They were an unusual pair: white-haired, jolly, not from around here, sharply assessing in their gazes. In my madder moments I would have them down as angels to my devil.

'Yes! Do you think it's still winter?'

He took a breath and grinned. 'Not today!'

She laughed.

'Enjoy your walk,' he said, firmly.

We are superstitious about the season's turn. You might wish it early but you would not call it too soon. Conditions in the 'Long Winter' of 1962–3 were described by the *Manchester Guardian* in March 1963: 'Troops relieved a farm on Dartmoor, which had been cut off by twenty-foot snowdrifts for sixty-six days.'

The view from the obelisk swept across the tree-tops to Heptonstall, the church above the Buttress, and beyond that to Stoodley Pike, and the fields rising to the moor tops and the sky. A haze-like shaken dust filled the valleys, and the sunlight seemed old, as though it had fallen out of the leaves of a book. On the high fields the snow lay along the hedge-rows, and there were horses in blankets grazing pale turf, and sun glinting off weekend cars, and the trees bare on all horizons, and light like silver webs on the near fretwork of the birches. The buzzard rose from below, rocking his wings up the unsteady air.

This! *This!* I thought. How did I let myself fall so far from this? All I had to do was hold it in my heart, take it as love, and give it as love. It is not so hard.

With my back against the obelisk, where the names of the war dead face the sun, I stood for a long, slow while. The Book of Common Prayer came to me unbidden. 'I have sinned against you in thought and word and deed, through ignorance, through weakness, through my own deliberate fault. I am truly sorry and repent of all my sins.'

You cycle around how honest is your repentance, how true your sorrow. Up there, in the tentative sun, I could hear no false note. I was as frightened as I had ever been. Sometimes it is like watching horror unfold across the sky in slow motion, while you stand paralysed in a dream.

Rebecca and Aubrey came back, and Robin later, and we had a lovely night. There was ease in the house like grace. I made the boys laugh and we all talked at once. Aubrey showed us his kicks after supper. (He is a red-belted ninja tot, learning discipline, self-control, respect and self-defence at the behest of a booming Black Belt, Master Ogden, who combines a spiritual air of uprightness and clean living with a commanding roar.)

If this winter gives me kindness and grace to give to them, then it will be a blessing.

19 FEBRUARY

Yesterday was a day of absolute grey stillness. In the afternoon Aubrey and I went walking. Under the cloud the world was perfect soft tranquillity. We held hands and talked of many things: our favourite animals; which dinosaurs we would be; Aubrey's imaginary puppy – name of Ace, colour white – and his current interest in what we are going to be after we die. He selected a weaver bird, or maybe a 'marine reptile'. In his mind these are bigger than plesiosaurs, of which he is also fond. I chose a whale. The valley was a fecund wreckage. You could almost see the nutrients scattered across the turf. The merest change in temperature now, the slightest spark of light, would fire the green fuses. The snowdrops were amazing, gorgeous white bells, fat as pearls in the moment of their perfection, hope incarnate.

'Look, Aubrey!' I said. 'Snowdrops! Spring will come.'

'Snowdrops!' he said, delighted with the word. 'What *is* spring, Daddy?'

Wood pigeons leaped up from a field below us and we discussed the eyes on the sides of their heads and the positioning of eyes on antelopes and sheep, versus on humans and other carnivores. In town he pointed at the ducks. They had eyes on the side of their heads!

Not winter and not spring, and warmer, and just now the tawny owl outside, a male: Whick! Whick!

Today the snowdrops have begun to open their petals, slowly lifting white arms from their sides like ballerinas. The first honeybee appeared, flew into the attic and caught its foot on an old web. I helped it out; it went and came back. Midges dancing, but more cold prophesied. A huge bell of warm air has lifted off over the North Pole, altering the jet stream.

Mum has had two old sheep die on the mountain; 'I like it when they die at home,' she said, 'no fuss.' One body was down to white bones in two days, the foxes, ravens, crows and buzzards banqueting.

Frieda and I went up to the obelisk at sunset, a red flash under a soft lid of cloud. As I carried Aubrey on my shoulders later, he wondered how ducks sleep, where water comes from and why we can't fly. A thrush called at twilight, the notes bringing the air to them so that the evening seemed to listen, and the thrush paused, listening to the quality of silence it had summoned to hear its song. Ducks flew up the valley in the gloaming, three together, flighting for the woodland pools.

20 FEBRUARY

A flying blue morning, England turned out in her winter best. Everything seems to rejoice under the sky and a sun warm for the first time. A Canada goose washes himself in the canal, plunging head and neck under, ruffling and splaying his wings, plunging again, vigorous with the cold, the light and the water. Two more pass over high up, giving their music to the valley. What wild sound is more wonderful than the turbulent, colloquial cries of geese? A ringing, chiming, honking clatter, it seems to hold such celebration and surprise, as though the world they fly over unrolls new and unsuspected beneath them. Magpies are busy everywhere. I think there is a trick in the old rhyme, 'One for Sorrow'. You almost never see a solitary magpie, they are compulsively companionable. Single magpies are half-joys: you count them as such and wait for the second to appear. The crow family breed early, as close to winter's teeth as they dare, feeding their young on the eggs and nestlings of the songbirds.

The train for London from Leeds has all of this British winter aboard. It was threatened with cancellation because of a fatality on the line near Hitchin, a person under a train.

Depressive thoughts must be most common in winter, but suicide peaks in the spring. It is not clear why – it is thought the surge in the light and temperature bringing hope to the world exacerbates the victim's isolation. We run south on time towards the scene of the tragedy, the train manager making the most of the microphone. His managers have menaced him with the consequences of inadequate information, so he addresses us loudly every few minutes. 'We are heading into uncertainty,' he says, and reprimands seven individuals standing in vestibules: 'Completely unnecessary,' he stresses, there are 183 available seats.

I wonder who it was at Hitchin. He or she walked onto the northbound track.

The fields are cold-yellow, piebald horses stand together as if waiting for a signal. Sun glints on the trackside stones and I think of Patrick Kavanagh, the inexhaustible wonder of a gravel yard, and Larkin: 'Where can we live but days?' We live in overlaps, normally, between hopes and anticipations, and present business. Our minds filter and tint the past, turning it so it catches the light; most involuntary memories are happy ones, most of the time, and so we are granted forwardness and direction. Depression, seasonal and otherwise, turns all this upside down: the past is a guilty place, the future a hanging threat, the present a humiliation. Stop it, you want to shout. Just stop it. Let me be.

Beyond the windows the light holds promises, hints of hope. The silver birches sing light back to the sun. Coots, tufted duck and mute swan bob on the lake wash of an east wind, bullrushes behind them flexing gold and feathered. On a fifty-acre field a hundred rooks feed and forage, walking into the wind. A joy of magpies rush a buzzard, all three of them low, hedge-height under the air. A solar-panel farm gazes darkly at the clouds, its feet in water. In a hundred flat miles in the middle of half-term there is not a child outside; a man talks to two Labradors at a field's turn, lecturing them, as they raise their noses and wag their sympathy. Pylons march into a westering afternoon as a swan beats his wings, stretching tall in a sugar-beet field, as if fanning four companions, snowdrop-white. Starlings! A hundred, no murmuration but a trace, a skipping wisp of a flock over the field's brow.

The settlements of the south-east, bald-brick and close-drawn, seem encircled in the wide land. Grantham's spire gives way to Grantham's Asda and Jewson and Tesco and Dunelm, High-Street Britain's bass beat. A raw, boorish day now, the grass greying under a thickening sky. Here are dream-green nitrogen fields, here umber tones in soil turning black as we southern. Dog-walkers pass under wind turbines and sillion glimmers in thick plough.

'We are approaching the area that has caused the delay,' the train manager says, 'the area of disruption.' Earlier he caught himself on the point of saying 'fatality' and changed it to the approved 'railway operating incident'. The deceased is purged from the account – a person, then a fatality, now an incident.

We pause at Hitchin, as if paying respect, then drift southwards, trains roaring by frantic for the North. Somewhere here, somewhere near the low roofs, in this outskirt town, someone crossed the little fields north of Stevenage – somewhere here. There is a lone magpie, rain spots on the carriage windows.

Outwardly we pay the world no mind, the winter no mind, and in the carriage a man sneezes and says, 'Bless me' in a tired way. And the fields dip and undulate now; to the south-west a yellow lightening and clouds heading up as if for sea, the edge of the lid, London.

On the way back the train rocks into Leeds, late.

'Better than the way down,' a man says.

'Delayed?' asks a woman's voice.

'Suicide,' he says. 'I was on the ten fifteen. It was cancelled. I don't know why people do it.'

'All sorts of reasons,' the lady replies, anxiously.

'Horrible way to go. Horrible for the driver,' he says. Then, with a bitter laugh, 'The tickets were really cheap so the compensation will be tiny!'

She says nothing.

'I'm so tired,' he says.

You can hear the tearing disintegration of sympathy for the victim, and the exhaustion, the money worry. It is a miniature of a country hardening to cold. The news has no relief for the North: we all know Brexit is going to bring us low. And yet – in Mytholmroyd at twenty-four minutes past eleven, on an over-lit and ghastly train, a tall young man gives two middle-aged women such a sweet smile, a one-corner-of-the-mouth lift of amusement and solidarity, as he makes way for them, and one notices me noticing and grins at me, and you think maybe, just maybe, some deep kindness among us will keep us together.

22 FEBRUARY

The cold has come back, a hard gripping. Lyndon, our neighbour, has set up an emergency feeding station, a dish balanced on the wall over the road. The birds are wary but the squirrels keen. At nightfall he is out, running his hand over the cars, checking for frost. 'Minus one, minus two,' he says, with satisfaction. 'I've got thermometers inside and out.'

There is an energising spirit in the frigid night, something perceived by a sense beyond the five, like a sparkle running through the bones. The tawny owls are busy, three at least, conversing.

Now the power cuts. I dash out to see if it is just us – but it is the world, the world transformed, released into darkness, moonlight, stars and frost. It is the first time I have ever seen our valley as it is in itself at night. Under a half-moon, with the hills' backs prickled with stars, its character has entirely changed. The dark no longer hunches around the few street lights. It is dimly luminous, stretching and languid, the moonlight a soft sweeping, rounding and gentling the ridges. The constriction of the valley is gone, the silvered fields wide under the mantling moon.

Candles, you think, and husband the heat, and go to bed before it gets colder. The winter of an older time, suddenly. And the power returns, and you thank goodness, though outside the lights are aggressively bright and the night's expansive soul has fled, bolting back into the past.

23 FEBRUARY

A pale-orange dawn and very cold, the birds slow to sing, their first calls tiny peepings. In hoar frost and sun the valley was motionless, breath held in the wide, pure smell of the freeze. Up into the wood we went, Aubrey poking the runnels, delighted by trapped air bubbles and white-starred ice. He was tremendous this half-term morning, climbing rocks, telling stories about sea planes and snow troopers, whipping through his letters. 'Which hand is the M in?' he demanded, hiding two behind his back.

Later the day hardened, the sun retired behind yellow-tinted clouds I associate with the coming of snow, and the trees stood motionless. The smell of the cold is fierce and distinct, local to each part of the valley. Here it holds hoar-frost grass, rigid moss, sheep fields, cold bark and that emptiness: the olfactory receptors in the nose retreat, leaving the icy flare of absence which is the smell of winter.

25 FEBRUARY

The light was astonishing today, the air whitening the sunlight, the cold burnishing the blue, the light like the absence of smell in the air, both bright and bleaching. There seemed to be no dapple, no interplay of shadow and light. In the sun there was a glittering, blintering blaze with a stark radiance in it. Out of the sun the shadows were scoops of cold, like darkness left lying in broad daylight.

Sometimes I feel as though I am coming back; the will is there, and the hope. Only the ability lags behind them. This ghastly ball of negativity, clamped to my ankle by a chain of self-loathing, follows me around. It is like being stalked by a ghoul. Turn your gaze outwards, I keep telling myself. You do not matter; other people matter, the land matters, the sky and the world. If only you would get out of the way of your own view!

The landscape has changed again; the snowdrops have paused, the shoots hesitate, the trees stand as if shocked – there is no ebullience in them: they give off a kind of introverted rigidity. They are working at a cellular level, dead cells freezing while the membranes of living cells soften, allowing water to pass into the spaces between them. In lower temperatures the liquid in living cells becomes glassy and viscous, preventing it from crystallising, preserving the cell in a suspended animation. In deep cold the trees become cellular jigsaws of frozen dead and liquid living. Perhaps this nuance of life and death in interplay explains the feeling in these winter woods.

The country is excited and alarmed, following the weather forecasters who speak slowly, tracing the path of a claw of cold reaching down from Scandinavia, spinning amulets of snow and ice on its wrists.

Contemporary winter has a distinct and speeding rhythm to it, thanks to advances in forecasting and the accelerating infotainment cycle. Sailors, the keenest weather-watchers, trust a three-day forecast and keep an eye on five to seven days. But a five-to-seven-day forecast is now given with more confidence than caveats: a three-day forecast today is more accurate than a forecast for tomorrow made in the 1980s, and seven-day predictions are now more accurate than five-day forecasts then. Forty years ago, NASA's computers analysed weather data at a million calculations a second. Its computations now run four billion times faster. The vertical structure of the atmosphere can be measured top to bottom, allowing analysts to read a complete temperature profile, which helps with the hardest prediction: the line between rain and snowfall, dependent on a line of freezing which may be on or far above the ground, which will rise or fall with local conditions.

When tomorrow's snow was forecast five days ago the news websites were the first to react, with radio, TV and then the papers following. The system was named 'The Beast from the East', and predictions of snow burial and catastrophe were made in the conditional tense. Two days before the first flake the NHS warned of the danger to the elderly, and the Society for Acute Medicine of the danger to the NHS. Now train companies warn of cancellations, the Highways Agency of poor driving conditions; the nation is told to 'check ahead', keep homes at eighteen degrees or more, wrap up, watch for ice. When the snow finally falls, commuters in London are urged to be home by 6 p.m. The media now solicit pictures and stories of the snow, cold and disruption which can be fed back into the narrative.

The spiral from fact (it will snow) to hysteria (flee for your homes!), from the hopelessly obvious

(keep warm) to exaggeration (the beast), from genuine care (the elderly) and quotidian alarm (the
trains – again!) to anticipation (yellow alert, amber
alert), to crisis (temperatures plummet!) makes a
whirling, see-sawing narrative.

Wallace Stevens saw that 'One must have a
mind of winter', being nothing oneself, to behold
'Nothing that is not there and the nothing that is'.
The poet offers the idea of winter as nourishment,
as stimulus, as a valued time, as part of a sacred
cycle in a post-sacred world. To behold it for what
it is, to read nothing reflective in it, to hold oneself both part of the cycle and apart from it seems
an act of everyday genius (according to F. Scott
Fitzgerald's definition, of holding two opposed
ideas in mind and still being able to function) which
modernity now imparts and demands.

The wonderful thing about savage weather is
the relief, in nuance, in which it is depicted and
discussed. With the world whirling faster towards
all its brinks, if you believe the news, there is an

honesty, clarity and proportion about the coming of hard weather. There is no schism in it, no enemy behind it, no trick to it, no fault in it.

As darkness falls, figures in hats and coats make for the Trades Club, where *The Vagina Monologues* is being staged for one night only. Queues of women, twenty to every man, line up the stairs. Something between a reunion, a demonstration and a carnival comprises the atmosphere; women are hugging, holding hands, laughing, watching and sipping drinks. The auditorium is a curving womb tonight, red-lit, decorated with paintings and designs of the narrow cave, the source of life, and ballooned, and soon warm. Rebecca is performing, shimmering in sequins and stage fright. The first speakers give their lines and immediately voices at the back demand they give them louder. And now they come, the stories of American women of twenty years ago in Yorkshire accent and form. Rebecca is brilliant. She draws the audience to her and has them shouting, reclaiming cunt, or 'coont', as she pronounces it, wonderfully. With whoops and applause, with gusts of laughter and standing ovations, with hisses and boos at the villains, with appalled silence at the worst of the descriptions, the hall and the performers become one body. There is no English reserve here, or male self-consciousness. This is something exhilarating, pagan and stormy, the feeling of a time in its tipping. It has been a winter of upheaval, as if a fierce, uproaring force is shattering upwards through rotten concrete. The wit and strength of the performers floods towards the audience, is met and answered. When the performance ends there is dancing, and shapes of women, men and spirits, people who are both and neither, no other thing than themselves, turn and twist under the lights.

27 FEBRUARY

Yesterday was the strangest day, snow blowing out of clear blue air. The east wind carried small messenger flakes far from their clouds, sending them tipping and stumbling horizontally, widely spaced apart in broad currents. At evening they came faster out of the east, pouring towards the sinking sun.

The storm arrived in the night, huge sticky flakes reaching for each other, teeming down. Minus one, two, three, and freezing air came in through the keyholes. The schools were closed, Hebden deserted. We had a snow day, watching the falls, practising our letters and reading. No post, no recycling, barely a car passed; three runners with a dog plunged through a heavy fall. The small birds were silent, only a slew of jackdaws rose over the wood, soot-dark, turning like flakes, rising. In late afternoon a tawny owl called; it seemed to summon evening early. The stillness of night lay on the woods though the light had barely dimmed. The fall was heavy and wet, three or four inches. It relented in bursts and fell again with more vigour. By nightfall it was minus five and the house seemed to contract, the fire hunching.

The layer of snow on the roof makes for a warm night upstairs. I wake at four, and get no more sleep thereafter. I miss being able to function. The smallest tests — rising, showering, shaving, preparing for the day, choosing clothes, preparing Aubrey's breakfast, doing the washing-up — come as monumental, exhausting waves. Each takes planning, takes resolution, is accomplished slowly through downpours of doubt and self-criticism. It is like a cruel and sardonic inversion of the idea of living in the moment, which is supposed to make you calm, or at least balanced. You live every moment as if it were a punishment.

I know I need to go to a doctor, but I am terrified of the consequences. They will tell me I am bipolar, and they will prescribe lithium, and I cannot, for all my searching, find evidence anywhere of a writer who made a life on the pills. Numerous accounts are of numbness, disconnection, endless tinkering with dosages, and suicides caused by people coming off it. Or perhaps it is only the fear itself that characterises this condition and these consequences in this way; I am not an objective judge of anything. I ricochet between fear of going to a doctor and guilt for not making an appointment. Hopeless.

I MARCH

Ferocious snow, the road impassable, me in Liverpool, and all the weight on Rebecca. She loads Aubrey into the sledge and tows him to town. Our friend Andy, father of one of Aubrey's school friends, looks after him, the school closed, and feeds Rebecca. She teaches, reclaims Aubrey and tows him back up the hill. She sounds alive with it all:

'We're fine, we're fine!' she laughs at my fret. 'Got the fire going, got food, we've got fish and pasta.'

Aubrey is in sublime form on the phone.

'Daddy, you know I bit Jonah?'

'This was two years ago?'

'I bit him and he punched me. When I was small.'

'I do remember. Why did you bite him, do you remember?'

'I was being rambunctious!'

'Oh yes?'

'Yes. I was being rambunctious for no reason!'

In Wales it is minus eight and Mum is snowed in. 'Just like the winter of '83,' she says. 'I got the stores in. I remembered powdered milk. Colin Brown moved the ewes down from the hill for me – I was worried about them for two days. I couldn't have got to them up there. I was thinking, well, is it better to go quietly with hypothermia, or the abattoir? But they're safe.' A neighbour took hay bales to her rams. 'If you look out of the window it's snow like dust devils whirling around the garden,' she says. 'I went out to feed the birds but it was just terrible. My hands went blue. Just like that! I said to Apollo, that's it, we're staying in. When it drifts the sheep can shelter behind them, but this is blowing everywhere.'

She is right in the teeth of it, Storm Emma from the south meeting this eastern beast.

That mountain winter of '83 we opened the front door to a perfect wall of snow; negatives of the planks, the door handle and the letter box were printed in a frozen wall. There were drifts in the attic, blown in under the eaves. The windows became opaque, obscured in a peculiar blue-white. Not far from the farm, exhausted after feeding the flock, Mum sat down to gather her strength. With a start she realised she had almost nodded off. She trudged her way back to the house. 'Look, children!'

she said as she came in. 'Icicles in my hair! I think I nearly died in the meadow . . .' As the drifts rose up the walls, blocking the door and covering the lower windows, she calculated our supplies and listened to the radio. 'They're saying make an H in the snow if you want help – but who's going to see us up here?' Mervyn, a neighbour, rescued us, battling up through drifts. He used a stake to dig out the top of the door. He was a tough and whiskery man. I saw his face widen with a delighted grin as he cut through the snow and found us. He hauled us up into a world erased, the fences vanished, the gates gone, the meadows overflowing the hedges. The whole mountain was moving, stalking down through the storm from the heights, the drifts in marching gangs.

My brother and I were evacuated, first to Mervyn's house, then to a friend's in town. Buried in drifts, the sheep ate wool off each other's backs. For a week Sally and Mervyn fought to dig them out and feed them. Not one was lost.

2 MARCH

The white deepening as you come into the Pennines is dramatic: three days' snow humped and frozen, the trees stark, darkly shocked, the roads glazed with salt dust and slush-swish, and everything sheened with ice. The cars carry hoods of old snow and icicles. In the Co-op people are marvelling at the empty shelves. 'I keep thinking if I walk by them again something will change,' a woman says. No veg, no bread, no eggs. The shoppers look bemused, and much happier than I have ever seen them, stimulated by the denial of the usual choice, grinning as they improvise. The normal Friday heaviness is gone. Small knots form, discussing options, debating other shops which might be open, might be stocked.

Aubrey and I play Snap, then Go Fish with invisible cards.

They are asleep now; Rebecca will be far under. She laughed at my fuss.

'We're Northern,' she says. 'It's just snow.'

The wind is busy outside, a hollow-sounding inrush, as though hard domes of air are pummelling the sky. The valley glowed blue-white at nightfall, the snow reluctant to give up its light. And the male tawny was back, he yickered twice, as if he had burned his feet.

I talk to my father about seeing a doctor. Last year I waited the blues out. This time they are worse. Something must change.

'But it wouldn't hurt, would it?' he presses, gently. 'They can't *make* you take anything. Wouldn't it be good to find out? Isn't that what we do – we go and find out?'

He is right. Of course he is right.

3 MARCH

Icicles hung in choirs, slush lay in runnels and an ice mist drifted over the valley, the world poised between freeze and thaw. Towing Aubrey on a sledge through the woods, we were escorted by two robins, then a wren – tiny troglodyte with her up-flicked tail! They must have been hoping Aubrey's charges through the undergrowth would expose some morsel, though spiders, beetles and worms surely went deep days ago. The colours are menacing, dark blue in grey in white, bands of suspended moisture, a sky washed with cold.

4 MARCH

Ice mist wisps up from snow on the valley floor and creeps down from the moors. A sinister silver darkness descends, ever so slowly, the mist thickening into night.

We have it relatively easy in Britain, even in winters as long and harsh as this one. In Krasnoyarsk, Siberia, my friend Mike waited forty-five minutes for a bus in minus thirty. When he first moved there he wrote of ice two inches thick on the insides of windows, and of being afraid to walk out of his father-in-law's dacha because of the bear population. On his way to work last week, in the middle of the city, he saw a boy attacked by a pack of wild dogs, then saved by a passer-by.

5 MARCH

With Robin home we have a lovely supper. Aubrey takes charge, making us play card games with invisible cards. Rebecca and I grin at each other over the children's heads, close in a way we have not been for a while. Robin is sweetly gentle with his brother.

In the night the roof starts leaking, not over my bed, for which I am prepared, but at the front, so that it pours straight down into the room where Rebecca and Aubrey sleep. The water is horrible, filtered through mould and soaked insulation wool. In the insulation space it is clear that all the battens and beams are rotten; the whole roof is surviving by habit. I get the tank from the bottom of the fridge and ease it into position. The water drops happily into it, in the torchlight, and stops running down to the room below.

6 MARCH

Sleet stalks about in the clouds but refuses to fall as I work on the roof. The local web is full of damage reports – boilers gone, leaks, burst pipes.

The nearest roofers are booked up until September, they say. Lyndon lends me his ladder and foots it. There is a thin strip of daylight visible from inside; I think it must have been partly blocked by moss, now torn off by the thaw. With the slate pushed back the gap is much smaller and I am praying that other gaps have not opened up. Wait for rain. Thank goodness for this journal. To have somewhere to put this small story, something to do with it, is a salvation. It is one of the few places where I feel any kind of measure of control, in this diary and in the lectures and seminars at work, which are going well, according to the students, despite my fears. Thank goodness for work.

7 MARCH

A beautiful smell, suddenly, this morning, something with turf and green in it, a fresh, plucking smell, as if the ground has borne some spirit of life. The last snow is a patch in the wood opposite. The kestrel came to the tree below the house, a small male, and the second honeybee of the year appeared. How on earth did it survive?

Late that night the stars are sublime in an icy clear. I lie awake again, much of the night, listening for the rain. It does not come. Instead there is more snow, great sticky flakes. The snowdrops push up through it as it melts, white parachutes opening above cloud.

9 MARCH

The rain comes. I listen to constellations. Soft as children's whispers at first, then tippling, then fatter taps. Aubrey's friend Wilf is staying. In the bedroom their breathing is perfect peace, gentle as nightfall. And the roof holds – miracle. All night the rain visits in different moods and modes, but nothing comes through. No storm-blown test yet, but there is hope. I wonder if fixing the roof is a turning point. Last winter, when I was similarly frozen inside, and useless, the handle on the back door broke. The moment I realised I could fix it by inserting a certain piece of Aubrey's Lego into the mechanism, something seemed to click in me, as in the lock. It sounds ludicrous, but I drew esteem from it: I am not utterly hopeless. I can cope! From then on things seemed to start to get better.

10 MARCH

Winter's cloak trails mist over the Pennines. Three herons row through it, towing time. On the high roads the snow lies like bodies, drifts contracting. The sheep look filthy and triumphant, survivors. I am fighting dark fantasies of the future, of failing as a writer, of losing the house to banks and bailiffs, of dragging us all down.

Worst of all are my fears for Aubrey, let down by his father, trapped by the geography of poverty. I picture versions of him in some dark alternative of the years ahead, angry and denied, throwing my advice and my warnings back at me: *Why should I listen to you? What did you ever do for us?* But there, downstairs, is the real little boy, who is so full of love and wonder and marvel, who is so rich in affection for people and enthusiasm for life, and my fears are ridiculous, a double betrayal. How hideously fast and creative is my mind in its formation of horrors and guilts; how rapidly it assembles evidence – from the news, from the world, from books – and how capably it constructs morbid and doomed conclusions.

There is a comical aspect to despair, too. My search history is a hypochondriac's encyclopaedia. I have a brain tumour, lung cancer, multiple sclerosis, chronic fatigue syndrome, motor neurone disease:

Google does not know what to make of me, showing me ads for making wills one moment and retirement portfolios the next.

Rebecca endures and endures my monotonous negativity. We both know it will end, but I am damned if I can see how or when.

II MARCH

Sun and blue, and the first breath of warmth in the air. Two grey wagtails hunt across the roof, flicking themselves in half-somersaults, a joyous canary-gold, picking among the mosses. We go up to the obelisk in the afternoon; it is still winter there, the wind ear-biting. There are snow lines lying against the hedges towards Heptonstall.

12 MARCH

A time to stop hiding. I make appointments with the doctor and a therapist.

'We can't breathe,' Rebecca said. 'Aubrey and I can't breathe.'

My panic is suffocating us. I cannot afford it, but I must. It is a time to try anything.

A counsellor with a medical background is available. Ellen comes from Germany; she made her life in the North after studying at Leeds. She is a trim woman with a searchingly direct gaze. Her office in the town hall is quiet and absolutely comforting. You can see why people would pay just to be here.

'I work for the NHS in Keighley four days a week,' she says. 'You have no idea of the things I see there. People with real, terrible problems. Yes, you have made mistakes. Yes, you have done bad things. So has everyone. Show me someone who has not. You have taken the first step by coming here.

A bad person would not want to change. You want to change. You should be proud.'

I know she is almost bound to say these things, but you feel something inside you uncoiling, slightly, as she speaks. We talk; I pour out my guilt and desperation.

Ellen draws a chain comprised of NC – NC –

'It's a bit CBT,' she says, 'but negative cognition – negative cognition, that's what you are doing. Look.'

She draws three lines, a horizontal, a wave and a jagged zigzag.

'I don't believe in a purely medical solution,' she says. 'I'm a psychotherapist, not a psychiatrist. I push you hard and you react – good. We make progress. Here are your moods. You have been on the jagged line. Perhaps you will never be on the straight one, but we can take you to this one, the wave, where you go up and down but not so much.'

'Do you think a doctor will help? I have an appointment.'

'Yes, you should go and find out. But you will be put on a waiting list, could be twelve weeks, could be twenty.'

It comes back to childhood, she believes. 'This need to be loved. This need for approval. This feeling that you are responsible for everything, from childhood, for everyone's feelings. You are so tied to these ideas. But a child should not be responsible for everything.'

'But I'm forty-four!' I protest. 'I should have gone to therapy twenty years ago!'

She laughs as I beg her for an assessment of chances of success.

'You are so scientific!'

'I'm really not. Fifty-fifty?'

'Better than fifty-fifty.'

13 MARCH

I travel to the Lake District, to talk at a festival in Keswick; the Pennines are dun-brown heaves, hessian-coloured. As we curve north there are snow lines, remnant bones in the angles of the high ground. Lambs run in the fields, which look drained and exhausted, as though all the life in the ground has jumped into the animals. At Keswick there is sun on the south flanks of Skiddaw and a fleeting warmth like cats' paws over the lake. 'It's been a hard, hard winter,' says John Lister-Kaye, a pen-friend met for the first time. 'Deep frost,' he says.

At lunch I talk with Linda Blair, a psychologist. We discuss the rising tide of mental ill-health, the plague of the age. In Liverpool I see staff with depression trying to teach students with depression, both sides incredulous, somehow, that we are all here, doing this. And yet the effort is valiant: we all fight on. In Finland last winter a sailor said to me, 'We're all going to need *sisu* now.' *Sisu* is a

Finnish word meaning a dogged and bloody-minded refusal to be beaten. I had assumed that the anxiety tide, which is particularly present among my students, must be related to the situation in which they found themselves. Studying creative writing, which offers no guarantee of a job or livelihood, and which confronts you with a great deal of darkness and fear – stories being a mechanism for the working-out and working-through of the difficulties and trials of life – must make their anxiety worse, I had supposed. But Linda says it is everywhere.

'I saw it at Bath Spa,' she said, 'students and staff. I'm having to cut down. So many patients. And now I'm interested in doctors. They are under pressure you would not believe. Some of them are cracking up and the rest are just holding on. They need help.'

The sky is a longing blue, clear in the evening, fresh as a broken chalk, streaked with soft light. The snow still lies, and it will not be gone in the morning, but you can feel the turn in the air.

16 MARCH

Winter will not surrender to spring; this is an in-between season, sun following snow in a glance. Return home filled with hope after an hilarious journey, our overexcited guard calling cancellations, re-routings, tentative plans, until none of us know where the train is going or where it will stop. The house is happy and gentle. Aubrey has a certificate of merit. Rebecca is going out. 'Why do you look so beautiful?' Aubrey asks her. Outside the temperature plummets. Bath and bed and reading – *Meet at the Ark at Eight* by Ulrich Hub. Aubrey loves the three penguins kicking each other, smuggling one of their number aboard the ship and discussing the existence of God. He has become suddenly Christian, singing songs about Jesus on his donkey going to 'Jerusa'. He sleeps sweetly. Lines of snow slide down the skylights.

17 MARCH

Sticky goose feathers, tiny hard powder and blurting blown snow, it is a connoisseur's winter day. The flash and change of the sky is quite extraordinary; in bursts it is spring for ten minutes, with birdsong and buds, then the light yellows, seems to age and harden, and the silver snow comes again, driving sideways, upwards, in helixes and vortices, dissident tribes of flakes pursuing their own migrations. A buzzard tumbles and rags through twisting winds. There are whitened clouds flying across whitened blue. In the tops of the beech trees jackdaws are actually shivering, their tails trembling in the wind. Silver light, pewter light now, with trees purpling behind the blizzard.

Walking Frieda, we are both spittled with a strange form of fall, lighter than hail but heavier than snow, white as mint, its weight all velocity. Later Frieda's humans dash for Lidl in Todmorden through a snowstorm like boiling steam. The shop is a small warehouse, overseen by a laconic and amused cashier. Ahead of us someone is having six bottles of beer and crabsticks for supper; a small, greying man in grey ahead of him is buying nuts. Just nuts. Back and bank up the fire. The snow comes beautifully and mightily now, tiny flakes all-conquering, sublime.

My Norwegian friend Reidun, a geologist, sends me a list of terms for snow. The valley is working through an entire Norwegian dictionary of different snows. We have had *korn av hagl* – hailstones – but what found Frieda and I earlier was *eiter* – small hailstones. It felt like *eiter*. *Snoflukse* we had at daybreak, large snowflakes, but currently the flying silence is made of *fjukr* – light falling snow. The steam on the way to Todmorden was *snofnugg*, snow dust.

More snow is forecast, but this must be one of the last winter twilights of the year. The trees stand solitary, individual, outlined against the white; when the temperature climbs next week they will thicken, their colours shared and spreading.

A bitter night falls, snow blowing thinly, the temperature freezing, and the sky with a distant hardness in it, a withdrawn, cold mulling.

18 MARCH

Glittering sun on the snow still lying, and the air blue and dashing. The beck shimmers in the sun and the birds are singing, the clear air magnifying their calls. I go to Stockton in the evening, to talk to schools all day tomorrow. The North East is a huge heave of housing and massive roads. It has been a hard winter here, Cath says, as she drives us between schools the next day. She is a librarian, a tremendous small woman ('I'm only diddy!' she says) who has raised her children, supported her husband, Chris, and now zips in and out of schools and libraries, bringing zest, books, laughter. 'My granddaughter said the mini-beast from the east is coming! The mini-beast! I had to tell her it wasn't a real animal . . .' We talk about the region's feelings, this winter. 'If they ran the vote again it would still be for Brexit up here. If you had a job at Nissan, and you were on twenty-four thousand, then you worked somewhere else and came back, they'd only offer you sixteen. That's because all the workers are Poles. That's it, you see. It's never going to change unless they offer us a better deal. But politicians tell their own stories, don't they?'

The schools are excellent; you can feel it as you walk into each. In one the library is a hut in the playground; in another, Cath says, it is a stretch of corridor. In a third it went from a room to a cupboard. But in the hut the children pour out their questions, their enthusiasms, their favourite books, the animals they love and notice, the birds they see, their ideas for stories. The class sizes are large, the skies are settled grey, there is no air in some of the buildings, daylight is shut out by blinds, the classrooms sealed and ill-ventilated, and yet here is the renewal of the world. Here is the spring, their raised hands like new shoots, their eyes as clear as hope.

20 MARCH

It is the first day of spring, according to the calendar, but by the time I reach Hebden the temperature is below freezing. Snow lies, blotching the woods with ghosts. The house is lovely, Aubrey still awake, chatting about rabbits and fish and what's that animal with long legs that hangs onto fish?

It does not feel as though the winter has gone, yet. The salt still lies thick on the road. The roof is holding, though the slates have yet to be tested by real rain. We are all well, and Aubrey and Robin are flourishing at their schools. Rebecca is running often, preparing for an ultra-marathon in June. She has been offered work she loves, teaching philosophy. Mum is relieved at the retreat of the cold, and sad that she is not lambing. She misses her annual battle.

I am coming through. In the margins of this journal I have been struggling to eat, to sleep, to work. With the return of the light I can feel this changing. With counselling, with the admission – the first time I have made it – that I do need help, has come change and hope. This diary has been a lifeline, a place to put the days so that none was wasted, a way to see and celebrate winter in all its shadows and lights. At the heart of this winter I have found a double spirit, a flame and a shadow. The shadow is fear; the flame, love. In many moments, these last months, the shadow has been stronger. I have not written down all the rows, the despairs, the heaviness of spirit; no reader could have enjoyed them. Memory culls them, anyway; I will remember Aubrey's laughter, Rebecca's grin and might, Robin's gentleness and resilience. Of all the seasons, winter draws us together. Its legacy will not be the shadow, but the flame.

EPILOGUE

On March 29th, having been referred by a GP, I went to see a psychiatric nurse. I felt as though I was flipping a weighted coin. Three chances out of four, it's heads and you are probably bipolar, and this is the beginning of a whole world of pills and ills. Tails, you just might not be. I was scared. I dressed and shaved meticulously, determined to present myself as sane. Because the upshot was unconventional, it is better not to name the centre or the nurse. The interview took place in a room like a basement. The nurse, an assessor, she said, of twenty years' experience, was very bright and very thorough. I liked her immediately: her long practice did not seem to have blunted her curiosity at all. Over the course of ninety minutes she asked questions and recorded my answers on a laptop.

'Have you ever heard voices?'

'No.'

'Have you thought of harming yourself or others?'

'I've wanted not to exist, to be dead, but I haven't seriously planned to kill myself.'

'Do other members of your family suffer from depression?'

'My sister and my father.'

'Are you comfort-eating?'

'I have been.'

'Is it hard to get up in the morning, to function?'

'It has been, really hard, but I'm doing it.'

And so on. We began with my childhood and up-bringing, worked through relationships and career; we paused over moments of manic behaviour and depressions. By the end of it she had enough material for an accurate short biography.

'So what have I got?' I asked, when it was done.

'You're not clinically depressed. You're not manic. You're not bipolar. You are going to see a therapist, and taking exercise, so you're doing the right things. You are cyclothymic – but we're all cyclothymic to some degree – we all go up and down. Look, I'm not allowed to say this really, but omega threes, fish oil – take 900 milligrams a day. And St John's Wort. Get some of that. And you're worse when you don't get sun. Take vitamin D and vitamin B complex. And look at this.'

She showed me an American website with a list of behaviours.

'Perfectionism,' she said.

I read the list.

'That's me. Every single one of those is me!'

'Right. You might want to get the therapist to address that.'

I want to hug her. I thank her profusely.

'How many of these do you have to do?'

'Two a day,' she says. 'I've cut down.'

'You worked so hard – thank you so much.'

'Take care,' she says. 'Good luck. And if you need us, you know where to find us.'

Out into sun and straight to the health-food shop I go. Omega threes are on special offer. For the first time in months I buy without counting the cost. At the till I pay and break into the pill bottles.

'Getting them down straight away?' laughs a woman in the queue.

'If they're going to work, madam, let's have them now!'

I neck fish oil and vitamin D and St John's Wort. Come on, life. Let's have you back.

On the way to the train I call Rebecca and tell her what has happened. 'I'm not mad,' I burble.

'Of course not. I told you, didn't I?'

'You did. Yes, you did.'

The train curves through birch woods. The slender trunks of the trees are silver-white, and the sun flashes through them, bright-dark, bright-dark, bright-dark, too quickly for either to register before it becomes the other. Dazzle and shadow, dazzle and shadow, but it is the light that lingers in the carriage, not the shade. It is very late this year, but spring will come. It will come.

Horatio Clare, 2018

ACKNOWLEDGEMENTS

This book springs from a conversation between Jennie Condell, who wanted someone to write about winter, and the great Benjamin Myers, who suggested I might do it. My huge thanks to them both. Jennie's inspirational enthusiasm, support and attention make her a dream of a publisher. When I tried to hide behind generalisations, Jennie teased out a true and accurate book.

It has been an honour and a pleasure to work with Pippa Crane, most patient and diligent of editors: thank you, Pippa. The gorgeous cover in your hand was designed by Dan Mogford. If you heard about this book by word of mouth or from something online or in the press, that was probably the doing of the amazing Emma Finnigan: any author she promotes is blessed indeed.

For dauntless help, support, advice, friendship and professional brilliance, huge thanks to my agent Zoë Waldie and Miriam Tobin at Rogers, Coleridge and White.

My rocks through all times, hard and gentle, are Sally, John and Alexander Clare. Thank you, dear mother, dear Dad and dear brother.

Without the support and deep friendship of Jeff Young, Helen Tookey, Chris Kenyon, Roger Couhig, Doug Field, Ellie Hunt, Phil O'Farrell, Emma Back, Nathan McWhinnie, Niall Griffiths, Debs Jones, Robert Macfarlane, Kevin Bohnert, Marge Mather, Richard Coles, Alison Finch, Laura Barton, Merlin Hughes, Ben Hardiman, Mo Bakaya, Rob Ketteridge, Peter Florence, Becky Shaw and Jay Griffiths my winters wouldn't have no springs. Thank you for so much, kindest friends.

As will be clear to the reader, this book is really an inadequate hymn of thanks and praise to Rebecca Shooter, Aubrey Shooter Clare, Robin Tetlow-Shooter and Jennifer, Emma, Christopher and Gerald Shooter. All my love and thanks to you. May your winters be beautiful, your springs bright, your summers unfading and your autumns rich and fair.